W9-BTI-808

RETHINKING EDUCATION
The Coming Age of Enlightenment

RETHINKING EDUCATION

The Coming Age of Enlightenment

by
Roger J. Williams

Clayton Foundation Biochemical Institute
The University of Texas at Austin

Philosophical Library
New York

Library of Congress Cataloging-in-Publication Data

Williams, Roger J.
   Rethinking education.

   1. Education—Philosophy.   2. Education, Humanistic—
United States.   3. Interdisciplinary approach in
education—United States.   I. Title.
LB1025.2.W52   1985   370'.1   85-21507
ISBN 0-8022-2500-4

Because of her untiring devotion and support,
I am dedicating this book, with gratitude and
love, to Phyllis, my wife.

We do not know what education could do for us, because we have never tried it.

Robert Maynard Hutchins

Hell is where nothing connects with nothing. I've always believed that education has to connect everything with everything in order to make an individual free.

Vartan Gregorian

Education has for its object the formation of character.

Herbert Spencer

A wise man knows about many things and how they are interrelated while a successful specialist follows the old adage—he continues to know more and more about less and less.

The Author

Contents

7

..

Preface

This book proposes that education at all levels move as rapidly as is possible away from a fragmented, disjointed approach toward a more unified approach which will be coherent and integrated instead of incoherent and compartmentalized. Nothing needs to be subtracted from our sciences and learning, but much needs to be added in the way of perspective and coordination. This will lead to true enlightenment.

This unified education will have tremendous advantages:

1) By fostering human understanding, this education will improve magnificently our ability to get along with each other—in families, schools, churches, and synagogues, and in different cultures and countries.

2) It will enable us to work toward the solution of human and social problems which currently we cannot even tackle because of our almost total lack of effective multidisciplinary research.

3) With this kind of education it will be far easier to learn how to take care of our bodies—prenatally, postnatally, and in adulthood—so as to achieve and maintain optimal health.

4)   By developing a core of non-controversial world-knowledge, we can knit the peoples of the earth together to a degree hitherto thought unattainable.

5)   This unified education, wholly compatible with science and the humanities, will help get mankind as a whole on the right track with respect to morality and ethics and will lead individuals to live satisfying lives.

6)   This education, with its concentration on human understanding and mutual appreciation, seems to constitute a sure way of preventing an atomic holocaust.

Can we ask for more? This book is for everybody.

Roger J. Williams

Acknowledgments

Among the scholars who have furnished staunch moral and intellectual support for some of my leading ideas are: The University of Texas professors Ira Iscoe (Psychology), H. Malcolm MacDonald (Government), L. Joe Berry (Microbiology), David L. Miller (Philosophy), John A. Wheeler (Physics), Harold C. Bold (Botany); also Roger W. Sperry (Caltech), President Norman Hackerman (Rice University), President Frank E. Vandiver (Texas A & M University), the late René Dubos (Rockfeller University), the late Philip Handler (President of the National Academy of Sciences), and President-Elect George Rupp (Rice University).

My colleague, Dr. Donald R. Davis, gave strong scientific support and understanding. Linda Davis Kyle offered several worthy suggestions regarding the make-up of the book. My photograph on the cover is used with kind permission of *Austin Homes and Gardens* magazine.

Most grateful thanks are due to Marguerite McAfee Biesele for her work as a valued "accomplice" in the production of this manuscript.

Roger J. Williams
June, 1985

11

Chapter I

Enlightenment Involves Gaining Knowledge—but Knowledge about What?

I feel strongly impelled to write this book. It tells of simple truths not explored before which can lead us directly into a new age of enlightenment.

I was brought up under unusual circumstances and in a family where being unusual was no crime. At various times in my scientific work I had become interested in unusual people and unusual phenomena—a man who could not detect the odor of skunk; a chemical which tasted bitter to some and was tasteless to others; the fact that after an ulcer operation I found that morphine, instead of putting me to sleep as it does most people, kept *me* wide awake all night.

After I came to the University of Texas in 1939, I became intoxi-
cated with a new but related idea: *Possibly every human being on
earth is an unusual person.* I visualized a vast human frontier of
unusual people, largely unexplored and unknown. After much study,
I wrote a book, *The Human Frontier*, which was published by
Harcourt Brace in 1946. Academic people had applauded Alexander
Pope's saying "The proper study of mankind is man," but actually,
precious little time and thought had gone into the study of real
people. Even at that time—since the 16th century, in fact—
convincing evidence existed that "everybody is unusual," since
bloodhounds reputedly could follow anyone's trail by smell, thus
detecting a distinctive body chemistry.

What initially was an intoxicating idea has become a sobering fact
important enough to influence every facet of everyone's life,
worldwide.

This book which I feel impelled to write concerns an age of
enlightenment. What do I mean by enlightenment? An enlightened
person does not stumble around in the dark. One who is enlightened
knows about his own capabilities and tastes and is aware of those of
others. An enlightened person knows how to make and keep friends.
He does not fight or try to kill his enemies but seeks to negotiate. An
enlightened man marries a suitable wife and an enlightened woman
marries a suitable husband. Both seek with intelligence to find occupations that will give them satisfaction. They recognize individuality
in children and do not expect them to be carbon copies of their
parents, brothers or sisters, or anyone else. They enjoy literature, art,
and music, and the fact of being alive. They know how to take care of
their bodies and how to avoid unnecessary illness and other calamities. In short, enlightened people know how to live with each other
with satisfaction in a realistic world.

We human beings have been on this planet long enough so that we
now should be living in an age of enlightenment. Unfortunately,
however, we fall far short. Our enlightenment, such as it is, consists
of bright spotlights that we can throw on many facets of the stage of
life but no floodlights making it possible for us to see the whole stage
in perspective.

We have enlightenment with respect to many fragments of life.
These fragments are of very limited value, like isolated islands. We

lack the kind of enlightenment we desperately need—the broad scope of understanding which will help us live together in harmony.

Those who are pessimistic and cynical about the world and its inhabitants are looking through spectacles which permit only fragmented vision. If we were to put on special "spectacles" through which we could see the whole of life (I will discuss this more fully later in the book), the world would take on a rosier hue and realistically we would see the solution to many problems. Our current education denies us the use of these special "spectacles," but a unified education would provide them.

For a world education which will help to solve human problems and to bring diverse people together in common understanding, we crucially need a unified education rather than our current fragmented education. This fragmented education, from the standpoint of perspective and coherence, appears to be in shambles and tends to promote confusion and uncertainty in the minds of all concerned.

The education we try to give our children and young people in elementary schools, high schools, colleges, and graduate schools is surely not all wrong. It has flexibility and makes room for many diverse interests. This is good—and in schools everywhere, young people learn *together*; this is a social experience and is much better than if each pupil learned only within his or her own pigeonhole. Despite these and other virtues, however, our Western education is a bits-and-pieces effort. It is sadly incomplete, disjointed, incoherent, and lacking in perspective. There are many bare facts, but far too little critical thinking about them and their relationships.

There is an enormous amount of knowledge which is available to us as human beings. This includes all of history—every significant thing we know that anyone has ever done, said, believed, written, or recorded. It also includes all the wonders of mathematics and the modern "sciences." In addition, it includes all of the languages that have ever been used and all the literature, art, and music that has ever been produced. This is vastly more than any one person can encompass even in a lifetime of study. This being the case, what kind of knowledge should we, the people, center on if we want to gain a superior education?

One answer might be, "Let everybody study only what he or she likes most." If we accepted this proposal and followed it strictly the results would be disastrous. Any person would find it most difficult to locate anyone else with whom he or she could talk intelligently on scholarly matters. We would all become separate "islands," which we are not. From another standpoint, there would be some logic in the contrary suggestion that "everybody study those subjects which he or she finds to be most difficult and uninteresting." This suggestion would lead to a leveling process and toward mediocrity in all fields. Neither of these two suggestions is worthy of serious consideration. A sensible approach to education, however, demands a recognition of the unity which exists in the human race. We have a *community* of interests.

This book proposes that we set as the prime goal for education *centering our interests on dependable, coherent knowledge that helps us understand thoroughly the complete environment and the diverse people who live in it.*

This is top-priority education of which everyone, even small children, should partake. People are always in trouble. We live in a trouble-ridden world where individual and mass underdevelopment, diseases, disintegrations, murders, and suicides persist. We need to know *WHY*. We all want a better world; improvement must rest on full comprehension of why the world is like it is.

The education of every small child begins shortly after birth. When one's eyes first open, the retinas receive images, but they are relatively meaningless; it takes an active brain to deduce their meaning, and a small child begins very early to "make sense" of what he or she sees, hears, and feels in the outside world. Unless his or her brain can "pull together" all the signals that arrive from the nervous system, and make sense of them, the child cannot progress in education. Typically, it does not take long for a baby to derive meaning from what he or she sees, hears, or feels. Babies usually understand the language they hear and adopt it as their native tongue, using it within a year or two. All of this involves coordination as an indispensable component of education. Altogether, the learning we achieve before "school" is enormous.

Shortly after I became four years old, I was sent to a country school. My initial Barnes reader started out this way:

> One, one, one, little dog run
> Two, two, two, cats see you
> Three, three, three, birds in a tree
> Four, four, four, rats on the floor

These four lines, each accompanied by appropriate illustrations, were an excellent start for my formal education. I learned from them a wee bit of arithmetic, spelling, sentence structure, biology, ornithology, rhythm, and poetry—all tied together in one coherent package. Also I received at least a hint about two physiological processes—running and seeing. Coherence characterized the whole lesson—arithmetic tied to rats, birds, cats, and a dog, spelling tied to meaningful words, and the meaningful words tied together in sentences in which there was rhythm.

In order for education to provide us knowledge about the world and its people, we need all our knowledge tied together, and we cannot get this coordination from a mere microscopic examination of every tiny part. All our knowledge needs to be collated and coordinated; human ingenuity must come into play in this process. The purpose, however, is clear: to unify knowledge and let the whole, including the insights, percolate effectively into our minds and into society.

The Latin word for knowledge is *scientia*, from which our English word "science" is derived. "Knowledge" and "science" in the broad sense are synonyms. However, for many people "science" has come to have mechanical and material-centered connotations which I would like to avoid in this book. "Unified education" and "world-knowledge," on the other hand, have no such connotations and, without these hidden meanings, constitute the fundamental basis for a new education everyone needs. I will use "science" as a synonym for "knowledge" sparingly, if at all. Every possible field of knowledge is worthy and valuable. *The prime areas of knowledge which reveal the nature of human beings and their total environment should be, from the standpoint of education, paramount.* Every discipline that presently exists can, if judiciously coordinated, contribute to this knowledge. *No other knowledge whatever can possibly compete in importance with that which concerns human beings and their environments.*

Chapter II

What Should We Do with Knowledge?— Digestion and Assimilation

In order to get the value out of our food, we must digest it, assimilate it, and incorporate the food elements into the cells and tissues of our bodies. Similarly, since knowledge is "food for thought," we must digest it, assimilate it, and incorporate its vital elements into our thinking before it can benefit us.

In my more than fifty years' experience as a teacher I believe I have never asked students, by implication or otherwise, to listen to what I had to say and to be ready to spew it back to me at examination time. Many thousands of times, however, I have made expositions and explanations expecting the student to *understand* and digest what I had said and be ready to apply the ideas to other appropriate situations. I have continuously felt that it does students very little good indeed to memorize material without thoroughly comprehending its meaning. For knowledge to be effective, we need to digest, assimilate, correlate, and incorporate it into our minds and into our thinking.

When a fragment of knowledge presents itself, we should think of it from every angle and fit it into the body of knowledge we already have. We should ask ourselves many questions about its meaning, interpretation, significance, and how it can contribute in any way to our knowledge of different aspects of life. If we do not do this thinking (digestion), we have not become educated so far as this fragment of knowledge is concerned. Too often this is precisely what happens in our fragmented attempts to educate. We try to fill our minds with an unsorted jumble of relatively useless, undigested fragments.

Until new thoughts become an integral part of our storehouse of world-knowledge, they are undigested. When we have assimilated new facts, we learn to live with them and they become an integral part of us. We are changed; we are not the same as we were before we grasped them.

When we study any phenomenon, individual person, or a group of persons in fragments, bit-by-bit, without digesting and correlating our findings, the exercise is largely futile. Digesting knowledge is something like solving a jigsaw puzzle; each piece may tell a small part of the story, but the full meaning becomes apparent only when the pieces are put together. Building world-knowledge is like writing a poem; each word may, of itself, be drab, but when the words are put together in the right way, the poem may be beautiful.

Education which consists of uncoordinated, specialized bits and pieces of knowledge, often indigestible, cannot be assimilated and hence is without value. Wisdom is what we need and it cannot be attained merely by consulting numerous specialists, each of whom may have a narrow, restricted view.

Mark Twain has reportedly said, "Show me a man who knows a great deal only about one thing and I will show you an educated idiot; show me a man who knows about many things and I will show you a genius." Competent coordinators in the field of education are scarce. Currently, academicians usually tend to stick to their own specialty

and leave it to someone else (or nobody) to look at related facts and
see their problems in perspective. This may be a good procedure from
the standpoint of gaining specialized knowledge, but it is a very poor
one indeed if one is gaining knowledge in order to live in today's
world with grace and satisfaction. Herein lies a dominant weakness
in our educational system. When we do not coordinate knowledge as
we acquire it, we can never gain perspective, and *most students do
not.*

Because we so often hand our students an "education" without
perspective, they become intellectually lost. They don't know where
they are, where they are going, or why. Sometimes they blunder
around year after year, searching for an "education" which is not
forthcoming. What they probably need most is to coordinate the bits
of knowledge they already have and see the world and its problems
with a truly organized perspective.

It is conceivable that an extremely myopic individual might spend
a lifetime studying the Grand Canyon of the Colorado inch by inch
and fail utterly to see its grandeur. Likewise, educators and scholars
who are extreme specialists are myopic and may never see the "grand
view" of world-knowledge as a whole. We too often encourage
students to study world-knowledge bit-by-bit without ever appreciating that it all fits together. One cannot grasp the Book of World-
Knowledge and its significance by reading snatches from pages 19,
41, 86, 111, etc.; one needs to digest and assimilate its meaning as a
whole.

We need to coordinate each branch of science and learning with
every other branch, but we rarely attempt this. Until this is done,
assimilation is incomplete. The dovetailing between the education
students currently receive in the physical sciences and that which they
receive in the "humanities" is atrociously lacking, as the Rockefeller
Foundation Report, *The Humanities in American Life* (1980),
suggests:

"The need to interrelate the humanities, social sciences, science, and
technology has probably never been greater than today. They con-
verge in . . . subjects requiring interdisciplinary investigation because
of their social and ethical implications. Whether because of frustration, misunderstanding, or indifference, however, collaboration among

humanists, scientists, and technicians is insufficient. In universities and in public life the impression persists that the humanities and sciences form two separate cultures, neither intelligible to the other. This impression indicates a fundamental kind of illiteracy. So long as it prevails . . . few people will understand the real areas of interaction or divergence among science, technology, and human values."

Too often the education furnished today is an indigestible jumble. Instead of the jumble, we should educate students to know that a sound psychology is basic to all economic science and political science, and, in turn, sound biology, chemistry, and other more exact sciences must form the basis for this psychology. In reality, social sciences, psychology, and biology depend upon each other; specialized study of these separate subjects, however, does not bring this point out, and students attain little in the way of perspective. One cannot fully digest and assimilate any fragment of knowledge without having some comprehension of how it fits into world-knowledge as a whole. Intensive studying of the fragments of knowledge is highly desirable, but this is no substitute for looking with perspective at a broader picture.

Chapter III

Seeking after Truth

It is not my purpose in this chapter to treat such philosophical questions as: What is *reality*? What is *consciousness*? What is *truth*? In my experience these words are impossible to define without using other words about as difficult to define as the original. My main concern has to do with acceptable realities. The earth, moon, sun, and other stars are examples of what I mean by acceptable realities. I do not think that these objects exist only in my mind or in someone else's mind. I accept the common-sense view that they exist regardless of how many minds there are to contemplate them. These examples, however, should not carry the implication that *only* material

22

things are acceptable realities. In my view, acceptable realities include mathematical principles, laws of motion and gravitation, and many other intangible natural laws.

There is certainly no fixed formula or recipe for success in seeking after truth. In many sciences experimentation is essential, and sometimes the experiments are elaborate and extend over a period of years. Preceding this experimentation, however, are the ideas which lead to experimentation. No one knows where ideas come from or precisely why ideas come to some individuals in relative abundance and why, to others, they are rarities.

Not always does the seeking after truth lead to experimentation. Shakespeare did not have a woodshed, garage, or any other place where he carried out numerous experiments, yet he was a discoverer of truth par excellence. He found and recorded in his plays a multitude of truths and insights into human nature and many other things which cannot be matched elsewhere. Shakespeare must have done a tremendous amount of observation and must have known many people more than superficially. He probably did not take notes on all of these observations, but rather stored them in his mind so that when he was writing he could bring them together and make sense of them.

The ability to store numerous miscellaneous observations and bring order out of chaos is probably one of the prime prerequisites for great discoverers of truth. When one does this, intuitions are commonly involved. Intuitions are often the basis for planning crucial and innovative experiments in the physical sciences.

Sigmund Freud, long before psychoanalytic Freudianism became so dominant in psychiatry, had an intuition or hunch that mental disease had its basis in biochemistry and that ultimately it would be treated successfully by this means. However, he was in no position to follow up on this idea; he had no special training in this area, and indeed at that time there was nothing definitive known about hormones, enzymes, and vitamins. He therefore let this first intuition fade away and adopted the idea that mental disease originates because of early childhood experiences. It is evident now that his first intuition, which also included a recognition of the importance of hereditary genes, was sound and highly valuable. His second, psychoanalytic hunch has been discredited sufficiently so that few present-day psychiatrists would wish to be identified as out-and-out Freudians.

About 1968, Linus Pauling, a noted chemist, had a hunch or intuition which may easily prove to be, from the standpoint of human health and welfare, the most valuable one arising from his extremely fertile mind. This intuition said, in simplest terms, "In treating mental disease, let's try to normalize brain chemistry." This would involve the use of no drugs, which are foreign to the body, but rather the use of nutrients or other substances which are normal constituents of the brain cells. A corollary to this idea is that if some organs other than the brain are involved in disease, they too should be treated, not with foreign drugs, but with nutrients and other agents which are normal constituents of these organs. When mental disease is treated or prevented using Pauling's strategy, this is called "orthomolecular psychiatry." When other ailments of the body are treated or prevented by the same strategy, this is called "orthomolecular medicine." Pauling's intuition was based upon a tremendous store of chemical and technical knowledge and has such a strong common-sense appeal that no one at the present time is in a position to minimize its importance. A large part of the truth behind orthomolecular psychiatry and orthomolecular medicine is yet to be brought to light by sophisticated experimentation.

Charles Darwin was a master discoverer of truth. He was typically not an experimenter, but he probably made tens of thousands of observations in the biological field and stored them in his notebooks and in his mind for future use. These observations were not necessarily entirely original with him, but he frequently manipulated them within his mind. His outstanding genius involved his ability to pull together an enormous amount of miscellaneous biological knowledge and unify it. He thought his way through all of his many, many observations and came to most interesting and provocative conclusions which no biologist since his time has been able to forget. If he had merely catalogued his observations and had not digested and assimilated them, all his scientific insights and learning would have been lost. His undigested observations would have been relatively worthless.

The thinking process must, of necessity, play an enormous role in the new unified education. Gathering facts is important, but if we cannot pull them together in our minds and make sense of them, the bare facts will be sterile. Seekers after truth in any field often have to work their way through a large mass of detailed facts before they find it.

The truth is not made up of isolated facts. It consists of facts that someone has digested, assimilated, correlated, and dovetailed. The new unified education demands that digestion, assimilation, and correlation of facts be stressed in the pursuit of world-knowledge.

Even very young children, by intuition, can discern the truth when presented repeatedly with visual, auditory, and tactile stimulation in a unified, orderly fashion. George Bernard Shaw said, "One only has to see *one* white crow in order to know that not *all* crows are black."

Chapter IV

The Grand Scheme of Nature; the Place of Individuality

The first and by far the greatest wonder of the world is the origin and development of life on the earth. If this had not happened, the earth would be a barren waste; not a blade of grass or a green leaf would be found anywhere. There would be no whistling of the wind through the trees because there would be no trees; neither would there be shrubs or weeds of any kind, and there would be no flowers. There would be no fruits of any kind, no grapes, no wine, no yeast, no alcohol. There would be no insects—no grasshoppers or grass in which they could hop. There would be no "toadstools" and no toads to sit upon them. There would be plenty of water around but nothing to drink it or to swim in it. Every sea would be a dead sea, and all the

26

oceans, rivers, and lakes would be devoid of living things. There would be no grain of any kind and nothing whatever to eat. Furthermore, there would be no coal or oil or gas in the interior of the earth. Lightning would flash, but nothing could see it; no fires would be started because there would be nothing to burn. Thunder would roar but there would be nothing to hear it. Except for the presence of water, the earth would be a wasteland, as the surface of the moon is. The famous "Seven Wonders of the World," all man-made, would never have been built if life had not come into being.

While the origin and development of life is the most unique and outstanding "wonder of the world," there was, preceding it, another remarkable development which we should mention—that of building the unique atoms of the chemical elements from smaller units. These specific kinds of atoms came into being, each with its complicated built-in set of instructions (rules of conduct), each kind being unique in internal structure and in its characteristics. The building of these elementary atoms before our earth took shape was a crucial part of the Grand Scheme of Nature and basic to the origin and development of life, which we will discuss further in Chapter X.

More than a million kinds of living things of every description fit into the Grand Scheme of Nature. However, there is one important restriction which applies to this development. Nature never develops an organism within an environment in which the organism could not possibly survive. In other words, Nature designs organisms to live in the environment in which they develop. Survival is by no means guaranteed, but a newly developed species always has a *chance*, using its own instincts and capabilities. While a caterpillar, for example, in order to become a butterfly, needs to get from its environment forty or more distinct and different chemicals, and cannot survive unless it gets all of them, it needs only to take in air and follow its instincts to devour green leaves in order to get every one of these essential chemicals.

Human beings, the high point in life development, belong in the Grand Scheme of Nature, and they developed in an extremely complex environment which we need to understand if we are to understand ourselves and adjust successfully to this environment. Included in this environment from which we build our bodies is a host of chemical substances: (1) water, (2) oxygen, (3) calcium, (4) magnesium, (5) sodium, (6) potassium, (7) chlorides, (8) phosphate, (9) iron, (10) iodine, (11) zinc, (12) manganese, (13) copper, (14) cobalt, (15) molybdenum, (16) selenium, (17) chromium, (18) fluorine, (19) vanadium, (20) nickel, (21) silicon, (22) arsenic, (23) tin, (24) valine, (25) leucine, (26) iso-leucine, (27) methionine, (28) lysine, (29) phenylalanine, (30) threonine, (31) tryptophan, (32) retinol (a form of vitamin A), (33) cholecalciferol (a form of vitamin D), (34) α-tocopherol (a form of vitamin E), (35) 2-methyl-3-phytyl-1,4-napthoquinone (a form of vitamin K), (36) thiamin, (37) riboflavin, (38) niacinamide, (39) pyridoxine (a form of vitamin B_6), (40) pantothenic acid, (41) biotin, (42) folic acid, (43) cobalamin (contains cobalt), (44) ascorbic acid, (45) choline, and (46) linoleic acid. All of these chemicals are essential to the life and health of our bodies and must be obtained from our environment.

Items 3 through 23 in this list may be considered "minerals." It is curious that we absolutely need tiny amounts of a number of chemicals which are highly toxic even at moderate levels. These include copper, cobalt, fluorine, iodine, molybdenum, selenium, and several others.

The eight amino acids listed next are to be found in our environment in combined form in various (but not all) proteins available from plant and animal sources.

The items from number 32 through 46 are all essential to our bodies. In the cases of items 7, 32, 33, 34, 35, 39, 46, the need for these specific substances is not absolute; other chemical substances similar to these (like other forms of vitamins A, D, and E respectively) can act as effective substitutes.

Are we ever in trouble in our adjustment to this chemical environment? The answer is, "Yes, certainly." There are several regions in the world which cannot support healthy human and mammalian life because there is not enough of item 10, iodine, in the native vegetation to supply bodily needs. There are also regions of the world (notably in China) where a lack of item 16, selenium, causes disease. Incidentally, there are also regions where the selenium is too abundant to support healthy life.

Human beings, because of their individuality, their complex nature, their complex technology, and the fact that they roam all over the earth and store food and transport it widely, have peculiar problems in connection with adjusting to this chemical environment. The essential minerals, amino acids, vitamins, etc., do not commonly occur in ideal proportions in any foods, and food selection for the maintenance of health is exacting and often requires intellectual abilities far beyond those possessed by other organisms. Human beings are in an environment where they have to use their intellectual faculties and their potential knowledge of science to cope with their environment with greatest success.

Beriberi is a disease primarily due to a lack of a sufficient supply of item 36, thiamin. In some rice-eating populations as many as 2 out of 100 of the population have died each year from this lack. It is probable that substantially all of the 98 who did not die had a deficient supply of thiamin which impaired their health to differing degrees.

Another disease, scurvy, is caused by an insufficient supply of item 44, ascorbic acid. It has been estimated that in the American Civil War 15% of all deaths were due to scurvy. Many who did not die of the disease would, in all probability, have had their health and vigor improved if they had had an increased supply of ascorbic acid.

Pellagra is a fatal disease which has been prevalent in at least a half dozen different countries and is due primarily to a lack of item 38, niacinamide. In the southeastern United States, where corn was a dominant food, from 1910 to 1935 about 170,000 cases were reported annually. Undoubtedly there was a much larger number of milder, unreported cases.

Rickets is a disease which has afflicted untold numbers of people, primarily children, and has caused serious impairment of bone development as well as other developmental difficulties. It is caused by a lack of item 33 (vitamin D, of which cholecalciferol is one form), but is complicated by inadequacies and imbalances in calcium and phosphate intake. If the mineral nutrition is good, the body needs only sunlight in order to produce, in the skin, the necessary vitamin D.

Kwashiorkor is a serious and sometimes fatal disease of children who are malnourished in a number of ways, primarily, however, with respect to the proper assortment of items 24 to 31, the essential amino acids. This disease is widespread in many underdeveloped countries.

All of these diseases have occurred because we have been ignorant

about our human environment and how to adjust to it. In all probability, many obscure, present-day afflictions which medical science
does not know how to identify or treat (and which are numerous
indeed) are due fundamentally to deficiencies and imbalances with
respect to the large number of chemical needs which we have attempted to list in our forty-six items.

In our technological advancement we produce, among many other
things, agents to control insects, etc., and these can enter into and
contaminate our food, further complicating the problem of adjusting
to our shared environment. Human beings, like other organisms,
have a *chance* to survive if they use their full faculties.

Environmental science, knowledge about an important phase of
the Grand Scheme of Nature, is, in many ways, poorly developed
even from the limited chemical viewpoint. Nutritional science has
not developed to the point where we are absolutely sure about every
specific need. Complicating the matter still further is the individuality suggested by Lucretius (96-55 B.C.) when he said, "One man's
meat may be another's poison."

For human beings, a completely useful environmental science
should also include expertise in quite a different realm. As members
of an intelligent population we need to be aware of the intangible
mathematical principles, laws of motion, laws of chemistry, etc.,
which permeate the universe. Lower mammals do not need this
expertise.

Speaking now of an entirely different kind of intangible, we commonly express the opinion that children, for example, need love and
affection, but we lack definitive information and insight into how
important these and other intangibles are in real life. Among the
other intangibles which children probably also need are attention,
recognition, communication, knowledge to satisfy their curiosity,
entertainment, humor, discipline, responsibilities, challenges, and
appreciation. We are far from expert in our knowledge of how these
intangibles operate. The role of "psychodes" (to be discussed in
Chapter X in this book) in cultivating character is largely speculative.
These psychodes are an important part of the environmental picture.

There is much more to the Grand Scheme of Nature than meets the
eye. Developing a totally useful environmental science is a step
toward an even broader concept—comprehensive world-knowledge.

A combined, coordinated study of environmental science, coupled with a study of human sciences, would go a long way toward making it possible for human beings to live happier and more productive lives.

Individuality is intricately interwoven into the Grand Scheme of Nature. Life could not have developed as it has if individuality were absent. If inheritance involved producing exact carbon copies, this would go on forever without change and no new species would come into being. Individuality exists in all forms of life, but understanding it is paramount in connection with *human* individuality. Each person is unique in hundreds of ways, and if we fail to understand this, as we often do, we are in serious trouble in our attempts to value and appreciate each other. The new unified education has as one of its prime objectives understanding people. This understanding has been an important problem throughout human existence, but up until about the 1940s a vital ingredient of this understanding was missing: namely, information as to how and to what extent so-called "normal" people differ from each other.

About this time, information on this point began to accumulate, and its importance began to be recognized. By 1951 the monumental but unsung work of Professor Barry J. Anson, of Northwestern University, was published in his *Atlas of Human Anatomy* (W.B. Saunders & Co., 1951). Through scores of examples it showed that anatomical variability is enormous and far-reaching. As an anatomist, Professor Anson failed to comment extensively about his remarkable findings; he was content to record the facts. While specific studies directed toward understanding the details and scope of human individuality have been relatively rare, it is clear now that every baby who comes into the world is a unique specimen in hundreds of ways.

The extensive, "normal," *anatomical* variations are now known to be found in the digestive tract, the respiratory system, the heart and circulatory system, the skeletal system, the muscle system, the nervous system, the reproductive system, the endocrine system, the lymphatic system, in all internal organs in the body, the special sensory apparatus of sight, hearing, touch, taste, and smell, and the brain itself.

In the light of these facts, it is not at all surprising that there is independent evidence that so-called "normal" people differ also in their physiology, biochemistry, and psychology. By no means do they see, hear, taste, smell, feel, act, have the same emotions, or think with uniformity. The biochemical variations are most profound and far-reaching and are documented, in part, in my book *Biochemical Individuality* (John Wiley & Sons, 1956; University of Texas Press, paperback editions 1969 *et seq.*). The fact that *Biochemical Individuality* was translated into Russian in 1960, Italian in 1964, and Polish in 1969 attests to the universal appeal of the concept of individuality. Americans must not ignore its overwhelming significance in every aspect of their lives.

The variations with respect to emotions, acting, and thinking are often of great magnitude and have been detected in the earliest months of life. Fundamental variations in metabolism (biochemistry) are genetically determined and may persist throughout life. The vast store of actual and potential knowledge in this area is not recognized, explored, or exploited in current education. This kind of knowledge does not fit into any of the fragments currently present in educational curricula. It involves *all* of the following fragments: anatomy, biochemistry, genetics, psychology; it undoubtedly plays an enormous role in such subjects as history, music, art, literature, etc. Its cogency cannot be grasped by any strict specialist in any field. *Because individuality belongs everywhere in education, currently it is adequately taught nowhere.* The new unified education stresses it as a vital part of the Grand Scheme of Nature.

Fortunately, modern technology is rapidly increasing its potentiality in this area. Computer science will be an invaluable tool in the study of individuality and its wide significance. For example, researchers from the National Institutes of Health, using automated analyzers, found distinctive and stable biochemical characteristics in blood samples taken repeatedly from ten individuals over a two-year period. Computerized "discriminant analysis" was able to recognize the biochemical "fingerprint" of each individual, which was also graphically shown by computer-drawn faces (see Fig. 1). In ways such as these, computers and other technology can greatly extend our ability to collect data related to individuality and to assess the exceedingly complex patterns which exist in different individuals.

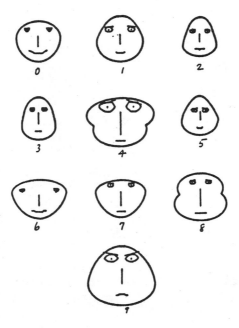

Fig. 1   "Faces" of 10 individuals in which various features are determined by 18 characteristics of their blood. (From "Biochemical Individuality and the Recognition of Personal Profiles with a Computer," E.A. Robertson, A.C. Van Steirteghem, J.E. Byrkit, and D.S. Young, *Clinical Chemistry*, *26*, 30, 1980.)

Chapter V

The Case for Unified Education
and for Cultivating Unified World-Knowledge

Before discussing some of the tremendous advantages of developing unified world-knowledge, let us consider problems relating to its feasibility and practicality.

Knowledge serves two important purposes. People, if they are hale and hearty, have a natural need and thirst for knowledge just as they have a natural need and thirst for water. Knowledge satisfies curiosities, but people are not merely curious about trifles; they are curious about the whole picture. The whole picture is what unified world-knowledge is all about. The second purpose which knowledge serves is that it makes it possible to answer questions and solve problems that confront us daily. This need is ubiquitous.

Unified world-knowledge is what a newborn infant begins to accumulate as soon as his or her eyes are open. This accumulation should continue through the years in school, and, after a few years, a child should have gained a great deal of unified knowledge that is indispensable to his or her life in the real world.

One of the important ways of attaining this end is to pay far more attention to the quality of material read instead of merely emphasizing the ability to read. If students read good literature of sound value, they will gain more knowledge with every page they read. The purpose appears clear: after a certain number of years a child should have accumulated—through reading histories, biographies, and works about other cultures, the progress of science and inventions, and many other topics—a storehouse of knowledge about the world environment in which he or she lives and the different social environments in which other people live. This accumulation of knowledge is the basis for development and for making mature and wise decisions in the future.

This increasing accumulation of knowledge should continue as long as one lives, and school days should by no means limit it. The accumulation of the right kind of knowledge on the part of its citizens is of vital interest to every community and to every country. We need public servants who are able to live their lives and do their work with satisfaction. We need citizens who not only will vote but will vote intelligently. The right kind of education is essential for everybody, and the right kind includes the development of all kinds of helpful knowledge. In our present culture there is essentially no coordination between human values and the numerous facts that can be known; therefore, the illiteracy to which the 1980 Rockefeller Foundation Commission Report refers prevails. We will abolish this illiteracy, however, when we fully cultivate unified world-knowledge. Children and adults (and certainly voters) need to know each day and at all times the basics of biology, of economic science, and of psychology. Unified world-knowledge includes all of these and more.

My fellow scientists have often remarked in casual conversation that anyone who can write about a field of science for children must be a master in that particular field. I envision the day when someone will be a good enough psychologist to write convincingly, for children ages ten to twelve, an exposition of what we *know* about psychology. If this cannot be done, I suspect there is something wrong with psychology. Someday an economist may be able to write similar material about what is known in the field of economic science. Indeed, it would be wonderful if someday a scholar could perform a synthesis and write a book on "Comprehensive World-Knowledge" for children this age. Such a book would also be invaluable to every adult.

It might be difficult to make a strong case for developing unified world-knowledge for everyone's use if the world and its affairs were entirely different from what they are.

The case is strong, however, because husbands and wives, for example, or other close associates do not always get along together and treat each other in a civilized manner, with mutual respect. It is strong because we do not know how to nourish and care for pregnant women so that their offspring are free from retardation, learning disabilities, autism, and other anti-social tendencies—in addition to many seemingly minor deformities which may have to be corrected by surgery in later life. The case is strong because we do not know how to train our children so as to prevent alcoholism, drug abuse, vandalism, terrorism, and assassinations. The case is strong because we do not know for sure how to prevent early heart attacks, premature senility, and strokes; nor do we have a good method of dealing with cancers in general other than by surgical removal or destruction. We need unified knowledge because of our present relative ineptness in dealing successfully with such diseases as multiple sclerosis, muscular dystrophy, arthritis, and schizophrenia.

We also need unified world-knowledge because the nations of the world frequently do not have friendly relations and are not content to have a wholesome "live and let live" attitude toward each other; furthermore, they often kill each other off in senseless wars based on avarice or differing ideologies, skin color, or religious views.

All of the distressing problems mentioned in the foregoing paragraphs are prevalent and widespread, if not universal, in the world today—and they are largely due to our lack of enlightenment. We can make at least a start toward solving every one of these problems and others by developing and disseminating unified world-knowledge and improving human understanding.

Whether our problems are interpersonal, developmental, educational, health-maintenance, psychological, occupational, economic, interracial, international, or of any other kind, unified world-knowledge will help in their solutions. Nothing short of unified world-knowledge will accomplish this end; specialized fragments of knowledge will not suffice. In other words, our present-day fragmented education does not pave the way for the solution of multi-faceted problems.

If they work at it, the scientists, philosophers, scholars, and educators of the world can develop and compile a compendium or an effective digest of all the non-controversial knowledge that we human beings possess. We can use this body of knowledge in many different ways. An adequate compendium should survey the complex field of knowledge, especially that which helps us understand ourselves, helps us make personal decisions, and forms a basis for our attempts to solve human problems. This material, certainly of interest to and suitable for students of high school and college age, will contain much that is *known* about basic mathematics, physics, chemistry, biology, geology, psychology, economics, ethics, anthropology, the polytheism of the Greeks and Romans, the monotheism of the Hebrews, Mohammedans, and others (as well as the views of disbelievers), and the lore of other ancient peoples. This survey should also include whatever is available in the way of penetrating biographies and histories, for these help us understand what people are really like. We should not neglect art, literature, and music, and we should *blend together in one unit the whole body of knowledge*. The survey will emphasize strongly what we *know* about these subjects and should be interesting and informative to everyone in every culture. It will leave plenty of room for speculation and differences of opinion about the multitude of things we do *not* know. This will, therefore, be far removed from a propaganda project.

If there are special fragments of total knowledge to which we have not given adequate attention for one reason or another, we need to correct this. For example, we need to know more about ethics—its roots, its importance, how to nurture it, and how it affects different people. Another area is that of aesthetics. Presumably all peoples have some sense of beauty, but does this sense have common roots? How is it developed?

It would also be very profitable to make a more thorough study of

humor—what makes people laugh and why. Why do things that
seem very funny to some people fall flat on other ears? When people
laugh they are usually not doing other things that are objectionable.
Maybe if we knew the Soviets well enough to make them laugh, we
would know them well enough to prevent them from such actions as
invading Afghanistan. It might be very constructive and revealing to
set up a humor contest between Soviet and Chinese Communists in
which two teams would compete to try to make their opponents
laugh themselves under the table.

There are probably many other areas in which our knowledge is
limited that would have a special appeal to other individuals. We
should explore every one of these areas and make the results a part of
the available education of all people. As investigative work develops,
new possibilities continuously arise, and certainly we should not
neglect them. I would like to see, most of all, a well-rounded education available to everybody. Everyone's knowledge will, of necessity,
be limited, but whatever a person knows should be unified, even if
diversified. This will be helpful in the answering of all kinds of
questions.

If we can successfully assemble a coordinated body of knowledge
of this kind and widely disseminate it so that it gets into people's
minds and into their thinking, this will be a magnificent, invaluable
contribution.

That blending and unifying different disciplines are not only possible but also actually being attempted is evidenced by a 1980 article
in *Psychology Today*, "Rediscovering the Mind," written by Harold
J. Morowitz, a molecular biologist. This is an *interdisciplinary* discussion of a number of fundamental problems. In it are to be found
statements such as the following: "Physical scientists are returning to
the view that thought—meaning mind—is one of nature's ultimate
realities." "If we envision our fellows solely as animals or machines,
we drain our interactions of human richness." "Primates are very
different from other animals, and human beings are very different
from other primates." "How remarkable it is that the scientific study
of the world led to the content of consciousness as an ultimate
reality." Without unified world-knowledge, the total content of this
article is difficult to discuss adequately because it involves the inter-

play of chemistry, physics, biology, and psychology. Regardless of the author's conclusions, the fact that he attempted to bring several disciplines together is outstanding, particularly because this is exactly what unified world-knowledge attempts to do.

We need fragmented science and have great uses for it. We also need, however, unified world-knowledge—the kind in which all parts coordinate with each other. Everybody needs to have a generous slice of unified world-knowledge because everybody has to make critical decisions which, without this kind of knowledge, they must make in ignorance.

More evidence that the intellectual world is moving in the direction of unified world-knowledge comes from the fact that the late Professor Fritz Machlup, an economist at Princeton University, wrote one volume and had projected seven more dealing with knowledge from A to Z, to be published by the Princeton University Press. This seems to be a step in the direction of unifying world-knowledge.

More evidence of the growing awareness of the importance of unified world-knowledge comes from the fact that in 1977 the Nobel Committee gave the Nobel Prize in Chemistry to Ilya Prigogine, not for his contributions to what might be called "straight" chemistry, but rather because he threw light on and contributed to a better understanding of biology and sociology. This rationale was unusual and unprecedented. Furthermore, the Rockefeller Foundation Commission on the Humanities Report certainly points in the direction of unified knowledge.

In addition to the four examples above, in Chapter VI of this book we will present our own brief Compendium of World-Knowledge to be absorbed during a common school education. This demonstrates, we believe, that it is possible to move at least this far even at this time in developing comprehensive world-knowledge.

Currently, some few scientists are giving biological psychology serious attention. We need to develop coordination between the different fragments of science in every possible way. I advocate a development not only of biological psychology but also of psychological biology, economic sociology, biological economics, psychological political science, economic geography, economic psychology, psychological and economic jurisprudence, and every other conceivable combination. When we coordinate each individual fragment of knowledge with other branches of knowledge we understand all branches better.

In view of the advanced thinking that has led to the article on "Rediscovering the Mind," and the fact that biological (genetic) psychology is receiving active attention, there is no telling how important unified world-knowledge may be when we develop it. It is highly probable that it will help us solve problems which we have hitherto considered unsolvable. We need to incorporate coordinated knowledge into our minds so we can think effectively about our real problems. This is especially true when we deal with commonplace but complex problems which have many facets.

The time has come when scientists and others must take unified world-knowledge seriously and develop it at every turn. It should be, for example, of major concern in our universities. It is good for everybody everywhere and at all times. If we should neglect to build up unified world-knowledge, one of the most poignant deficiencies in our civilization will be the inability to produce through our educational system great men and great women.

We have geared our educational system toward the production of great specialists but not great, statesman-like individuals who are able to attack any human problem with knowledge rather than whimsy. Historically, many of our greatest men and women have arisen from *outside* academic circles. We have not learned how to train great individuals. We can train and encourage the development of great men and women only by concentrating on unified world-knowledge and making its insights available not only to adults but to children at a very early age.

Even with our present knowledge and equipment there are several immediate moves we can make in the direction of developing unified world-knowledge. One of these involves a suggestion which I made in my book *Free and Unequal* about thirty years ago: "Start teaching children, even as early as the preschool years, about their own individuality. Even at an early age their senses of taste and smell, their reaction to colors and art, their ways of doing things, and their likes and dislikes in stories, etc., will be sufficiently diverse as to be striking and revealing." This would constitute an early conditioning, paving the way in later life toward an understanding of others whose sensory and intellectual equipment may be highly distinctive and different. In all human relations we need to know far better than we now do what people are like so that we can communicate with them and deal with them with honesty and integrity. No kind of knowledge that we can gather can be more valuable than this kind, and if children get early clues to this, it will be highly advantageous to them and to the people they encounter.

Another move we can make immediately is to teach that biological economics is for real. Contrary to some careless opinions, this is not a world in which there is "plenty of food and shelter for all." No one is *entitled* to a rose-garden existence. As John Kennedy once reminded us, we need to think more about what we can do for our country and less about the benefactions our country is to bestow on us. In the entire biological world (including human beings) no organism can go merrily on its way with the assurance that it will always have plenty of food and live in a good environment.

Another move we should make in the direction of developing unified world-knowledge is to see that every educated student learns something about chemistry. There are several reasons for this. One reason of outstanding importance lies in the fact that we cannot understand the essence of biology without this basic knowledge.

As we have already noted in Chapter IV, there is a vital and indispensable *chemical exchange* which takes place continuously between human beings and their environment. If we do not get from our environment into our bodies the right chemicals in the right amounts, we cannot live or remain healthy, so we should know something about these chemicals and why they are necessary.

We human beings cannot escape the population problem, and even if the earth were 100 times as large as it is there still would not be plenty of room and food over the centuries for a population that doubles every few decades. These are facts that all people must face squarely. No country *owes* its citizens *ad infinitum* standard living conditions.

People need to raise their sights and get away from the idea that material needs are the ultimate in importance. People need proper food and shelter but they also need—if they are to be healthy—knowledge, hope, love, friendship, and many other things of a non-material nature. People may be poverty-stricken in many other ways besides having a small or non-existent bank account. One of the reasons for moving toward unified world-knowledge is so that we can better fulfill *all* our needs. Science that deals only with material things cannot satisfy us completely, so we must replace it with unified world-knowledge.

In order that we need never call students "educated idiots," we need to give them a more rounded education. About fifty years ago the University of Texas instituted a "Plan II" which sought to accomplish this purpose. This plan stated that superior students did not have to have a specialized major but could get a more general education than would otherwise be the case. Thus, a trend toward a broader perspective in education has been "in the air" for several decades. The University devised Plan II partly because it would give pre-medical and pre-law students better preparation than a more specialized education. The institution of this plan came about, at least in part, through the influence of Robert M. Hutchins, of the University of Chicago, who advocated the development of courses of study which would allow students to go their own way at their own speed and to get a more general education.

Robert M. Hutchins was one of those rare men of influence who were not afraid to think and act boldly with respect to educational problems. Too often "educators" are content to ride along with the status quo and draw their salaries without worrying about fundamental problems.

Because Robert M. Hutchins lived when he did, he might not have been anxious to accord women the status they deserve, but I feel sure that if he were alive today he would heartily endorse the common-sense idea that the attainment of unified and coordinated world-knowledge should be a prime goal of every educated man and woman.

Every modern scholar realizes that human problems have many facets, and every competent thinker recognizes that in order to understand or solve these problems we must by all means develop breadth and avoid narrowness and nearsightedness.

If we who constitute modern society spend our money wastefully producing an inferior type of education, sooner or later we will have to pay for our folly. We cannot afford a bungled type of education, neglecting the unified, meaningful education which is just around the corner.

Now we are ready to discuss some of the outstanding advantages of the new unified education which embodies coordinated world-knowledge.

1. This new unified education will offer to young people for the first time in the history of mankind indispensable knowledge about the two prime factors which enter into every person's life: a) one's self and b) one's total environment.

Even the wisest and most capable men and women we know of in history have lacked the advantage of this prime knowledge. Education in past centuries and up to the present has ignored individuality and thus has taught a person virtually nothing about himself or herself as an individual; and because it is fragmentary it gives only an incomplete smattering of the *total* environment in which a person has to live. Our present-day, fragmentary education thus misses to a distressing degree the two prime factors of life.

Knowing one's self and one's total environment (which can come about *only* through the new education which stresses individuality) is important because this knowledge will help avoid the universally prevalent misfits of life, large and small—misfits in education, in occupations, in avocations, in marriages, and elsewhere throughout our society. Misfits in education include training for occupations and professions which one never follows, training for nothing whatever, neglecting a musical education when talent exists, neglecting an appreciation of literature when it might bring unbounded satisfaction, etc. One is lucky these days if there are no misfits in his or her occupation. Work should be for enjoyment and satisfaction; in such cases, within limits, long hours should be more satisfying than short hours. A good education should include knowledge about many thousands of occupations and how individual people may be fitted for them. Certainly, a central purpose of education is to pave the way for each educated person to earn a livelihood with satisfaction while cultivating his or her inner life. The new unified education is unique in that it aims to do exactly this.

Mismarriages, involving persons who with different mates might be very satisfactory husbands or wives, cause innumerable broken spirits not only for the adults but also for children. These mismarriages could largely be eliminated if the participants had the advanced knowledge about the individuality of themselves and others which results from unified education.

2. **Unified knowledge will give all civilized peoples of the world a foundation for common understanding and an indispensable basis for valuing, appreciating, and cherishing each other, and for cultivating goodwill. What this unified education can do for individuals it can also do for different cultures.**

This knowledge will provide for the citizenry of all countries a common ground of understanding on which to base their thinking, negotiations, and dialogue. Total environments in different cultures vary, and this new education will help people to understand their environment *in all its aspects* far better and to make the most of it whatever it may be. They will be in a much better position to lead healthy lives—healthy biologically, healthy psychologically, healthy economically, healthy ethically, and in every other way.

It is often said that troubles between nations are largely psychological. This may be true, but psychology is not built on vacuums; it is built on what is already in people's minds. If we establish, all over the world, a core of *non-controversial* knowledge, this will be a solid base upon which unity can rest. Psychological conflicts would become far less frequent. We will have more to say on this subject in Chapter VIII.

3. **Unified world-knowledge will help solve numerous and diverse health and other day-to-day problems.**

Unified world-knowledge has even wider applications than those we have mentioned. If there is such a thing as a panacea for the prevention of human ills and the solution of human problems, coordinated, comprehensive world-knowledge is that panacea. If, for example, one is constipated, has an itchy skin, a runny nose, or a stopped-up nose, he should go to unified world-knowledge to find out what causes these ailments and then contrive to eliminate these causes. If one desires to prevent something more serious—like a heart attack—the recipe is the same: find out the factors that might be responsible for heart attacks and eliminate them, if possible, from the scene.

One of the clear-cut advantages of developing unified world-knowledge, which includes more than a superficial knowledge about our environment and our bodies, is that by this means we can promote health and prevent disease. The U.S. Department of Agriculture has estimated that improved diets would result in 25% less respiratory disease, 25% less digestive disease, and 50% less dental disease. One can debate whether these estimates are accurate. I have presented, in *Nutrition Against Disease* (Pitman 1971, Bantam 1973), a great deal of information regarding the background of these estimates. The cost of medical care in our country alone runs into hundreds of billions of dollars annually, and if we could save a substantial part of this it would constitute a signal accomplishment and would benefit all citizens and all taxpayers. We must have a better, unified education if we are to learn how to prevent disease.

In my book *Nutrition Against Disease* I have called attention to the probability that many human diseases arise because we do not put the right things into our bodies when we carelessly consume attractive and tasty foods and leave out a consideration of their chemistry. Heart muscle, which works continuously day and night and in a healthy person pumps several liters of blood per minute for many decades, needs to get from the environment forty or more chemicals in about the right proportions, and heart failure probably often occurs because the food we eat, with its mediocre quality, supplies this assortment of chemicals imperfectly. Our knowledge in this field has not been comprehensive enough—we have paid too little attention to the chemistry of nutrition—and we are still in the twilight with respect to exactly what the nutritional imperfections may be in individual cases.

Of course, there should be no expectation that each individual will be an expert in this field, and one who wishes to prevent a heart attack should consult a physician who has substantial knowledge about nutritional and other factors and can give helpful advice. Unfortunately, medical science has been backward in this area. One of the early ideas in this regard was that cholesterol consumption plays a dominant role in producing heart attacks and that one should avoid cholesterol. The best medical opinion holds now that this idea is incomplete and that we have to look elsewhere for other crucial factors which precipitate heart attacks. Almost everyone agrees that cigarette-smoking is one of the "risk factors" and that we should avoid it. There is substantial agreement also that judicious, regular exercise is an important expedient in preventing heart ailments. Certainly we do not have information that would rule out nutritional deficiencies as a cause of heart disease. More and more evidence is accumulating that faulty nutrition, including nutritional deficiencies, plays an important part in the production of many minor and major diseases.

After I had discovered and synthesized pantothenic acid (see U.S. Patent No. 2,414,682), experimenters fed pigs a diet deficient in it. During post-mortem examinations, these experimenters found the pigs' gastro-intestinal tracts were ulcerated from one end to the other. This does not prove, of course, or even indicate that pantothenic acid deficiency is always the cause of ulcers, but it does show that *a single nutrient deficiency can cause extensive ulceration.* It suggests strongly that nutrient deficiencies of one kind or another can cause ulcers. So, if a person wishes to avoid ulcers, one important thing to do is avoid nutritional deficiencies.

If a person wishes to take all possible steps to prevent another type of malady—mental depression—he or she should also avoid nutritional deficiencies and imbalances; niacinamide deficiency, for instance, can even cause insanity.

As we have already noted (p. 24), in 1968 Linus Pauling, twice a Nobel Laureate, initiated and promoted the idea underlying ortho-molecular psychiatry, that using chemicals which are natural to the body rather than chemicals which are completely foreign to the body is the best means of preventing or curing mental disease. In other words, completely successful nourishment of the brain cells will cause them to be healthy, and the mind will remain healthy.

Medical scientists have long known that immunization procedures can prevent smallpox, yellow fever, poliomyelitis, and several other diseases, and this is an area where medical science has made relatively great advances. The nutritional prevention of disease, however, is relatively in its infancy and we have much unified knowledge in this field yet to explore.

The study of nutrition is one which inherently calls for unified knowledge and which fragmented science has neglected. Nutrition involves chemistry because chemicals are what we need to get in our food; it involves physiology and cell metabolism—these are crucial factors; nutrition also involves psychology, because nutrition may greatly affect one's psychology and personality; nutrition involves genetics as well, because one's genetic background greatly influences one's quantitative nutritional needs. Economic science is an important consideration in nutrition since cost is a basic factor in determining the availability of food. Unified knowledge is therefore absolutely essential to the proper study of nutrition.

Because fragmentation of science has led us to neglect nutritional principles, we have promoted some diseases which otherwise would not have existed. One of these is alcoholism. In a pre-publication edition of my book *The Prevention of Alcoholism through Nutrition* (Bantam Books, 1981), I wrote the following words, which speak for themselves:

> To Medical Professionals: The Alcoholism Problem as Seen by One Who Appreciates the Intracacies of the Nutritional Process
>
> Some people are highly vulnerable to alcoholism, while others are not. There is nothing unusual about this. This is true of many other diseases—diabetes, heart attacks, ulcers, tuberculosis, arthritis, and many minor troubles like graying of hair and balding.
>
> So far as nutrition is concerned there are two basic facts to be considered. First, the cells and tissues of our bodies require a complex environment in order to live and thrive. Oxygen we need minute by minute. We have some storage capacity for water and many other items, so we do not have to replenish our supply so often. At the beginning of this century we knew very little about what our bodies needed. Now we know there are over forty distinct chemical substances (minerals, trace minerals, amino acids, and vitamins) each of which is absolutely essential to our lives, and if our cells and tissues are to function well, we must obtain these environmentally in about the right amounts. Secondly, because of the complexity of this inner

environment and the many balances which must be maintained, practically speaking, there is no such thing as perfect nutrition. Our bodies
are adaptable and many people, including those in America, live their
entire lives getting nutrition of only mediocre quality. Ideal or perfect
nutrition is out of the question.

When a vulnerable person starts to consume alcohol, he or she does
not start at the highest nutritional level but more probably from
basically poor or mediocre nutrition. The drinking of alcohol thus
tends to make poor or mediocre nutrition even poorer. If drinking
becomes regular, and especially if it becomes heavy, the internal
environment (IE) of the cells and tissues of the body deteriorates
seriously for two reasons. First, consuming alcohol crowds out of the
diet many important life-giving chemicals and secondly, because alcohol itself in higher concentrations is poisonous, it pollutes the internal
environment in our bodies. When heavy drinking continues, one's IE
becomes worse and worse and many regulating physiological and
psychological processes controlled by the brain and the nervous system fail to operate successfully. In the hypothalamus of the brain there
are appetite-regulating mechanisms which become impaired. Normally, people desire food and nourishment, and the mechanisms in
our bodies operate to satisfy our needs. When, however, a person
becomes addicted to alcohol, these mechanisms are deranged and the
individual may become nauseated by the sight or smell of food. Only
alcohol is attractive, and it can satisfy only temporarily.

What we all need to learn is that our IEs are all-important, and that
these inner environments need to be built up rather than depleted.
Very few people, if any, can afford the "luxury" of immoderate drinking at any time. Heavy drinking always precedes alcoholism.

We need to attack the problem of alcoholism *long before* it becomes
an accomplished fact. Even before alcoholism presents itself as a
possibility, people should do several things which will not only head
off alcoholism but help prevent many other health disasters. People
should (1) eat more sensibly, (2) moderate their consumption of
alcohol, (3) take regular exercise, (4) get adequate sleep, and (5) build
up a wholesome attitude toward life. Building up one's IE involves and
reinforces all of these measures.

A crucial question is this: When does one or when should one learn
about the importance of IEs? The sooner the better. If one learns this
as a youngster and is taught to regard his or her body as a temple of
God, this is excellent; if one learns this before drinking patterns are
established, this is good; if one does not learn this until after he or she

has become an alcoholic, this is *bad*. Even worse is never to learn it at all.

The importance of IEs in the prevention of alcoholism does not in any way deny the importance of psychology. We seldom emphasize as we should, the importance of the nourishment of brain cells. That on the average brain cells are often poorly nourished is indicated by the fact that brain cells die at the rate of about 2000 per hour even in supposedly healthy adults. This is an *average* estimate. In alcoholics, brain cells must die off much faster; often medical students cannot use the brains of alcoholics after death for dissection because they may have largely turned into structureless mush. It seems obvious that the brain and the brain cells have a great deal to do with alcoholism and the psychology of alcoholism.

Our bodies are marvelously built, but they are not compartmentalized. Anatomy, microanatomy, physiology, biochemistry, endocrinology, emotions, and drives are all closely intertwined. If we guard and build up our IEs, we have taken a long step forward in bettering ourselves. Preventing alcoholism is only one phase of a grand scheme for human betterment.

As we shall see later in our discussion, we need to attack social problems—crime, delinquency, racial hatred, and war—following the same strategy: first find out, using unified knowledge, the roots of these troubles, whatever they may be, and then contrive to eliminate them. We should take for granted that these problems are complex and that all social science disciplines enter in—psychology, economics, ethics, etc. For this reason, only unified knowledge can give us the answers we need. If, as some would contend, we are totally unable to develop unified knowledge, we may have to live indefinitely with these calamities. If, on the other hand, we *do* develop unified knowledge, we may become relatively effective in preventing crime, delinquency, racial hatred, and war.

Unified knowledge is indispensable to a well-rounded education; it will foster the development of human stature and human character; it is our most important resource for solving human problems and cultivating understanding and amity among people of the world. We *must* develop it.

4. Unified knowledge will make possible bringing into the world babies equipped with maximum potential.

In the January 1981 issue of the *Proceedings of the National Academy of Sciences*, some of my friends published the results of an exploratory experiment in Norfolk, Virginia which gives a strong, if not certain, clue as to why 3.2% of the babies born in our country are seriously mentally retarded. As a result of preliminary experiments it was postulated that if we supply retarded children (even several years after birth) with an abundant assortment of nutrients we can partially abolish their mental retardation. This postulate was supported by the Norfolk experiment. Every one of the children who received the active supplement had his or her IQ rating raised, whereas those receiving the placebo were unaffected.

This study strongly suggests the desirability of finding out whether other childhood aberrations—hyperactivity, dyslexia, childhood schizophrenia, seizures, etc.—may not also have their roots in prenatal nutritional deficiencies.

As we have pointed out, it is recognized that about 3.2% of the babies born in this country are regarded as seriously mentally retarded. It may seem extravagant to say so, but it may nevertheless be true that, from a more comprehensive, enlightened point of view, as many as 32% or even 80% of our children may be "retarded" to an appreciable degree.

Many experts who are familiar with the problem do not regard IQ measurements very highly as true measures of intelligence. Several years ago I spoke to a national convention of Mensa, in Houston, Texas, a group distinguished by the fact that in order to be a member one must have an IQ of at least 140. I pointed out to them, as adroitly as I knew how, that there were many other signs of intelligence besides those associated with success in schoolwork—being able to handle money successfully, participating in happy marriages, bringing up children of high character, being skillful politically, being a skillful writer or speaker, being witty, etc. My talk was deflationary instead of inflationary. In spite of its faults, however, IQ measurement constitutes one way of measuring intelligence.

The Norfolk, Virginia study suggests strongly that the nutritional environment furnished by pregnant women to their fetuses can be markedly improved, and that if we develop unified knowledge so as to improve pre-natal nutrition as much as possible, the day may come when a child now given an IQ rating of 120 will be regarded as a retarded child, or at least on the borderline.

IQ measurements are, of course, only relative, and having an IQ of 100 merely means that the individual is about average with respect to what the IQ tests measure in a given population. If the whole population on which the IQ tests are based is careless with pre-natal and post-natal nutrition, the average intelligence might be low enough so that it would be uncomplimentary to say to a child, "You have average intelligence." If a particular child made a test score of 100 when compared with a population that was nutritionally careless, his or her test score might drop to 60, 70, or 80 if compared with others in a population which carefully provided excellent pre-natal and post-natal nutrition. In other words, if we want to do the most for children, we will probably want to aim much higher than "average" intelligence. A child now regarded as having average intelligence may be, in terms of the ideal, definitely retarded.

One reason for my enthusiasm about the potentialities of improved pre-natal nutrition is the fact that we *know for sure* that it works with animals. It has been shown that nutrition which "gets by" with adult animals may be far too poor to support healthy reproduction. This has been shown to be true for mice, rats, dogs, cats, chickens, turkeys, fish, foxes, and monkeys. It may safely be assumed that it would apply to humans as well. In some specific cases where a crucial nutrient is fed at different levels to animals, the number of deformities is inversely related to the amount of that nutrient that is made available.

Several years after we synthesized pantothenic acid and made it available to scientists, French investigators furnished different amounts of the vitamin to young female rats to see how different levels would affect their offspring. When very little was given no young were produced at all; when the amount was increased, there were a few young produced but half of them were seriously deformed. When the amount was increased still more, the litters were about 95% normal in size and there were very few deformities. While the investigators in this trial underestimated the need for pantothenic acid and did not give the optimal amount (along with all other needed nutrients), the optimal amount would have probably resulted in completely normal litters and no deformities.

Dozens of experiments have shown that relatively mild nutritional deficiencies at critical times during gestation may cause all kinds of deformities in every part of the body, including the heart and the brain. Sometimes poor pre-natal nutrition causes animals to be produced which have their brains outside their skulls!

In animals, we know that superior nutrition approaching the optimum consistently causes the birth of completely healthy specimens. Experiments involving giving highly superior nutrition to pregnant women to see if reproduction is markedly improved have never been adequately performed.

Because nutrition has been neglected in our fragmentary education, and because we have not grasped the idea that a lack or imbalance with respect to any mineral, amino acid, or vitamin can cause serious trouble, we probably give our puppies, kittens, pigs, and chickens a better start in life than we give our children. The widely used commercial cat, dog, pig, and poultry feeds are all conspicuously better balanced than are the foods that we, the people, eat.

The production of a baby with maximum potential is a complicated, intricate process. It begins wth conception—the fertilization of an egg cell by a male sperm. Inheritance is a very important and inescapable fact of life and is determined at the time of conception; it may limit one's potential. However, most of us have far more potentialities than we cultivate. Hence, we should not place too much blame for our shortcomings on heredity.

Associated with the Institutes for the Achievement of Human Potential, based in Philadelphia, there are schools where they have demonstrated that even "brain-damaged" children often have outstanding potentialities which can be cultivated.

Also, in Chicago, Marva Collins, an enthusiastic, enlightened teacher, has demonstrated that "underprivileged" children from the lowest stratum of society can be transformed into pupils who exhibit a tremendous thirst for learning and literature. As students, they often surpass those who have the advantages of the "very best" schools.

At the beginning of the life of every child (at conception) an intricate plan or blueprint begins its existence. The building process begins immediately and proceeds smoothly as long as the blood of the pregnant woman brings the needed raw materials to the site. The required raw materials include oxygen, water, and forty-odd chemicals in varying but appropriate amounts. The blood of the pregnant woman may also bring to the site harmful chemicals which disrupt the building process. Whether the blood brings the right things in the right amounts and whether it brings harmful poisons all depends upon what the pregnant woman allows to enter into her body when she eats, drinks, smokes, or takes injections. Since most people eat and drink carelessly, pregnant women as well, there is no assurance whatever that the growing fetus in the pregnant woman's body will escape poisons and get the nutrients it needs in optimal amounts. We need to bear in mind the statement made in the conservative *Heinz Handbook On Nutrition* (McGraw-Hill, 1959, p 137; reprinted with permission):

> It is often taken for granted that the human population is made up of individuals who exhibit average physiologic requirements and that a minor proportion of this population is composed of those whose requirements may be considered to deviate excessively. Actually there is little justification in nutritional thinking for the concept that a representative prototype of Homo sapiens is one who has average requirements with respect to all essential nutrients and thus exhibits no unusually high or low needs. In the light of contemporary genetic and physiologic knowledge and the statistical interpretations thereof, the typical individual is more likely to be one who has average needs with respect to many nutrients but who also exhibits some nutritional requirements for a few essential nutrients which are far from average.

For genetic reasons this applies to individual fetuses as well as to children and adults. Since the supply of some of the nutrients is likely to be suboptimal for a growing fetus, his or her total environment is suboptimal. Many babies who pass for "normal" have many structures in their bodies—in their circulatory systems, respiratory systems, urinary systems, digestive systems, etc.—which are far from ideal. A large percentage of patients in children's hospitals are there because of the need to correct deformities which may not appear to be serious but which nonetheless may present problems. These slight deformities may arise because the mother's blood did not furnish the right materials at the right time.

If the cultivation of unified knowledge would accomplish only one thing—giving the babies of the world a better start—it would be worth pursuing. At present we neglect to do this and nothing in our fragmented education suggests that this objective should have high priority. It can be achieved only by careful consideration of the entire environment during a child's growth and development. This environment includes not only the detailed nutritional environment discussed in Chapter IV, but also the intellectual and intangible factors which enter into their development. Recognizing the art of developing a child's intelligence and character demonstrated so remarkably by Marva Collins is perfectly in line with the new unified education everyone needs. This art can doubtless be cultivated, but not without the utilization of unified knowledge. The art could certainly not be developed as a result of narrow specialization. Marva Collins herself must be an extremely perceptive woman and this perceptiveness is probably an essential ingredient of the art. Whether men can cultivate this art as effectively as women is problematical.

5. Comprehensive world-knowledge will help greatly to solve intercultural, interracial, and international problems.

Whenever two or more persons discuss matters of mutual interest and concern, each of the parties involved is a unique individual in many ways, as we have explained near the end of Chapter IV. They are distinct and different anatomically, physiologically, biochemically, and psychologically. Because of many "normal" variations, their primary senses are not identical.

Since their endocrine systems are distinctive, they do not have the same emotions, and probably because their brains differ in fine structure and in the number and distribution of the various types of nerve or brain cells, they do not even think alike. Confronted with the same facts they do not draw the same conclusions, or do so at the same speeds. Problems which seem easy to some are unsolvable for others. Things that seem very funny to some seem not funny at all to others. An idea which seems obviously true to one may seem obviously false to another. Some individuals may be very clear-cut in their thought and expression; others may be evasive and seem to agree when really they don't.

In a conference, everyone has some tendency to conform to the pattern of those surrounding him or her, but everyone has an inalienable right and some compulsion to be himself or herself.

These facts and many others are among the ABCs of personal relations. These innate differences are in addition to those brought about by cultural differences.

Whenever two nations (or other kinds of groups) have problems to discuss with each other, the discussions always involve unique individuals who represent them. Any diplomat who fails intuitively or otherwise to recognize individuality must be a dismal failure. The more diplomats and others know about individuality, which exists within all races and cultures, the more able they are to communicate successfully with each other. When individuality is fully and widely recognized through the dissemination of the new education, *every* kind of negotiation becomes more profitable.

6. Unified knowledge will satisfy human curiosity and help us understand the Grand Scheme of Nature to a degree impossible when in our education we merely produce specialists rather than enlightened people.

Someone has remarked that certain problems seem practically insoluble until someone stops and thinks about them for a few minutes. This is one of those problems. It is simply preposterous to think that our curiosity about the world and the people who live in it can be satisfied by careful scrutiny of many bits and pieces. Unified, coordinated knowledge is so obviously essential to satisfying this broad curiosity that the mere mention of the fact is enough to carry conviction.

7. Unified knowledge will close the long-standing gap between science and the humanities.

Historically, we have broken science and all world-knowledge into different disciplines, each one of which is a fragment of the whole. In order to become proficient it has been necessary for individuals to be specialists and to concentrate their attention on some fragment, perhaps even a small one. This specialization is essential for the

development of the various aspects of knowledge, and every special-
ity must continue to receive attention.

One development needs to take place which is new and innovative.
This involves coordinating the different fragments of science into a
whole, coherent body of knowledge. Because of necessary specialization, this has been difficult, and because it has been difficult we have
neglected it. It is an obvious fact that many scholars who are proficient with respect to one fragment of knowledge are far from expert
in other areas outside their specialization. Competent coordinators
are scarce.

Scientists for example, need to take seriously and examine very
critically such questions as these: "Is our chemical science based on
thoroughly sound physics?" "Is psychology built on a sound biology,
and is biology well coordinated with a sound psychology?" "Does
our biology fit in with sound mathematics, physics, and chemistry?"
"Does economic science take into account sound biology and sound
psychology?"

The difficulty in answering these questions lies in the fact that
specialists often have limited perspective. For example, those
acquainted with the frontiers of physics are not likely to be
acquainted with the other frontiers. And the experts in psychology
are probably not in touch with those who are exploring in the field of
molecular biology.

The gap which exists between science and the humanities which
has been discussed by the late C.P. Snow and in the 1980 Rockefeller
Foundation Report on the Humanities is deplorable. But the answer
(seemingly the only one), which may be difficult to implement, is
extremely simple and can be summed up in three words: *unified
world-knowledge*.

**8. If in the whole world of knowledge there are as many as fifty
distinct disciplines, each one of the fifty will be enriched by coordinating it with other disciplines.**

We have illustrated this earlier in this chapter. I have learned about
the enrichment of one discipline by another from firsthand experience, and there is not a shadow of a doubt in my mind of its validity.
As a biochemist—one who is interested in the chemistry of living
things—my competence in the field has been enhanced by my knowl-

edge in related fields: mathematics, physics, organic chemistry, inorganic chemistry, physical chemistry, biology, microbiology, genetics, etc. If I were, at this stage, determined to increase my competence in biochemistry, my plan of advance would be *perfectly clear*. I would get a better grasp of mathematics, physics, physical chemistry, quantum physics, quantum chemistry, thermodynamics, atomic structure, genetics, and physiological psychology. The same principle of reinforcement applies to other fields. I cannot imagine a minister, priest, or rabbi who would not be a more competent minister, priest, or rabbi if he had a better grasp of history, economics, psychology, and biology.

I cannot imagine a political scientist who would not be a more competent political scientist if he had a better understanding of economics, psychology, and human biology. Any journalist would automatically become more profient as a journalist if he knew more in the fields of economics and social psychology. Lawyers and judges would be more competent as lawyers and judges if they were to have an improved understanding of psychology and human nature. Almost endless examples of this kind can be cited.

I estimate that the expertise of specialists in every field would be increased at least 100% by attention to unified world-knowledge. After unified world-knowledge is developed there will still be plenty of specialists. We will need them. But they will be far more competent specialists because of the breadth of their learning. A multitude of innovations will arrive simply because the innovators will have much more knowledge on which to base their intuition and their thinking. Common sense will be added to their armamentarium.

9. Unified world-knowledge will open the door to a sane and enlightened approach to religious ideologies and idealism.

In our present culture, whether we want to recognize it or not, our secular colleges and universities (which dominate education) do not teach students how to handle religious problems but actually encourage them to leave religion out of the picture. By and large, they effectively teach students to disregard the motto "In God We Trust" and to lead their lives as though God did not exist. The existence of a moral force in the world is more often regarded as relatively harmless superstition than a reality. Non-controversial world-knowledge must, of course, be neutral with respect to sectarian religions, but, unlike material-centered science and education which are largely oblivious to religion, world-knowledge leaves the door open and gives individuals a substantial basis for deciding what their attitude toward religion will be and what their preferences are.

Despite all the condemnations that have been placed at its doorstep, religion has been valued highly by millions, perhaps billions of people. Any education which closes its door to exclude religious idealism should not be tolerated. The new unified education leaves the door wide open.

Religiously inclined people may be among the most sophisticated and erudite people who have ever lived. In the Encyclopaedia Britannica (15th Edition, 1976 [Macropaedia], Vol.2, page 261) is the following statement:

> . . . the progress of science has brought man to a deeper and more precise knowledge of the magnitude of the universe and of the complexity of its laws (especially in the fields of microphysics and microbiology); but according to such eminent 20th-century physicists as Max Planck, Albert Einstein, and Werner Heisenberg, man merely discovers these laws, and they presuppose an infinite intellect.

While the existence of God has never been *proved* in the traditional sense, scientifically such existence is by no means a preposterous hypothesis. A good education should prepare us to discuss the proposition intelligently. This cannot be done on the basis of a fragmented education. It *can* be done on the basis of the new unified education.

10. The emphasis on unified world-knowledge will elevate the status of teachers, teaching, and education in the public mind.
More brilliant and dedicated men and women will be attracted permanently to the teaching profession; the profession will have a strong humanitarian appeal. The public will understand, endorse, and support more wholeheartedly this new education which leaves room for religious idealism and seeks for the whole truth, in preference to a fragmented education which turns out specialists who merely know "more and more about less and less."

The public, which has more perception than we sometimes credit it with, has never been enthusiastic about narrow specialization and "educated idiots"; these have little commonsense appeal, and the public cannot understand them. However, the public *can* understand and appreciate the new unified education and its desire to educate people in *every way.*

A PROPOSAL TO PROMOTE UNIFIED WORLD KNOWLEDGE AND PEACE

There are fourteen objectives toward which we, as individuals, should continually strive:

1. Attain and recognize as much non-controversial knowledge as possible.
2. Become more objective.
3. Gain greater ability to think through issues, to see alternatives, and to make wise choices.
4. Increase our ability to communicate effectively with others.
5. Enhance our ability to elicit cooperation.
6. Learn how to negotiate diplomatically.
7. Think positively in the direction of agreement rather than disagreement.
8. Understand and appreciate one's own individuality.
9. Understand and appreciate the individuality of others.
10. Cultivate greater respect for oneself.
11. Cultivate respect for all life.
12. Recognize and appreciate the importance of unseen forces.
13. Coordinate in our own lives human values and knowable facts.
14. Improve the quality of our reading material to gain wisdom.

Chapter VI

A Brief Compendium of Unified World-Knowledge

One of the first things which a newborn infant learns by observation is that meaningful sounds come from the mouth and not from the eyes, ears, or nose. Small children learn very early in life that we see using our eyes, hear using our ears, and speak and eat using our mouths. This is non-controversial knowledge about which no one will argue.

As a child progresses in his or her education there should be a continuous building up of this kind of non-controversial knowledge; it is vital that we as individuals build up this kind of knowledge and distinguish it from ideas and thoughts about which there are wide differences of opinion.

By the time a child has passed the twelfth year of life, he or she should have built up a tremendous store of knowledge. Some of this a child learns in school and some by common-sense observation—water runs downhill, light travels in straight lines and you can't see around a corner without a mirror. They should continuously learn to use words, hopefully with full comprehension. This does not always happen. The words "million" and "billion" are often used carelessly. We can better comprehend the meaning of the word million if we realize that to count to a million at an ordinary speed (to 100 ten thousand times), a person would have to count steadily for over 4 weeks, 40 hours per week. To count to a billion would require a steady job for over 80 years!

In the material I am about to present, I outline briefly the kind of coordinated knowledge (information) that I think everyone with a common school education, everywhere, should have. I intend it to be non-controversial—the kind on which all informed, educated people, regardless of their cultural background, will agree. Obviously, in compiling this, I have not consulted representatives of many different cultures, so what I have written is a mere first approximation; we need to mull it over and improve it, and if it is not completely non-controversial, we should make it so. We can extend such a Compendium, when circumstances and purposes demand it, to include far more detailed knowledge.

The Compendium

The following Compendium is significant because:

(1) The statements of fact we present in this Compendium are non-controversial from the standpoint of knowledgeable people, and are hence dependable.

(2) An intelligent teenager can understand everything in this Compendium.

(3) Despite its simplicity and non-controversial nature, this Compendium presents from six to ten potent insights—some of which are crucially important—about which the vast majority of college graduates are unfamiliar. This tragic unfamiliarity is due largely to the fragmentation and the resulting lack of coor-

dination of our science and knowledge as our educational system presents it.

Moreover, I take the firm position that very frequently, if not universally, students passing through our educational system fail, because of lack of perspective, to get a large part of the most important information which they desperately need. I did not invent or "make up" the information this Compendium contains. Competent scholars can search it out, but up to now they have not presented it positively and effectively and in proper perspective.

Disaster will result if we do not build up in our children and in ourselves a sound body of dependable, non-controversial knowledge.

Unified world-knowledge encompasses all disciplines—all kinds of knowledge. *Knowledge* includes everything we know, but does not include speculations, surmises, or fanciful ideas which we may entertain. The best criterion I know of for distinguishing knowledge from beliefs, surmises, and speculations is to accept as knowledge only that which all reasoning people will accept without controversy.

All kinds of knowledge are of interest and we should not overlook any of them. However, there are some kinds of knowledge which will be of more concern than others because they obviously relate directly to human problems we desperately need to solve. For example, if there are some peculiarities in the makeup of Saturn's rings, this knowledge is interesting, but unless it touches human life and human thinking in some significant way, we will regard it as low-priority knowledge. While we do not wish to hazard omission of any kind of knowledge from unified knowledge, at this stage of our development we will not deliberately seek to avoid pragmatism.

About the Earth, Sun, Moon, and Stars

The earth is a huge, roundish ball about 8,000 miles in diameter (a little less than 13,000 kilometers). It spins around its axis every day and circles the sun every year. This causes us to have night and day, and because of the tilt of the earth's axis, we have the seasons. The moon is a satellite which follows the earth and circles it at a distance of about 240,000 miles and shines only by reflected light from the sun. We do not know why the earth has only one moon, nor why some planets have no moons and others have several. We do not know why Saturn has rings around it while most of the planets do not. Of course, there is room for speculation with regard to things we do not know. In our solar system the sun furnishes most of the energy. On earth we get much of our energy *directly* from the sun. The fuels that we burn have derived their energy indirectly from the sun through the process of photosynthesis, which has taken place for millions of years. The sun is about 95,000,000 miles away from the earth. Light and heat from the sun do not travel instantaneously. They travel about 300 meters every millionth of a second and they require about eight minutes to travel from the sun to the earth.

Our solar system with its 9 planets is about 7 billion miles across but occupies only a tiny speck far from the center of the cluster of suns which we may call "our galaxy." This galaxy includes some 10,000 million suns with whatever satellites they may have. The size of this galaxy is incomprehensibly great. We can gain some idea of its size by imagining our entire solar system as being the size of a pinhead. On this tremendously reduced scale, the star nearest to our sun would be about 12 feet away. The other 10 billion stars are irregularly scattered through space at similar distances from each other and make up the whirl which, on our tremendously reduced scale, would be about 40 miles across.

While we have this reduced-scale picture in mind, we should also consider that outside our whirl of stars there are at least 100,000 other similar whirls of stars extending out (still assuming that our solar system is the size of a pinhead) to a distance of about 2.5 million miles.

Spectroscopic analysis of the light and other radiations coming from the most distant galaxies tells us clearly that these galaxies are made up of elements such as we know on earth. The universe therefore exhibits remarkable unity, not only from the standpoint of mathematics and physics but also from that of chemistry.

On the earth we find distinctively what we call living things— plants, animals, and others. We can *speculate* about the probable existence of living things on other planets, but we *know* about living things only as they exist on earth.

One extra advantage of astronomical study is that it tends to cause people to look at things in broader perspective.

All of this material regarding elementary astronomy has its basic roots in human curiosity. If we human beings had not been curious about the earth, moon, sun, and stars for centuries this knowledge would not be available to us. To satisfy human curiosity we have developed mathematics, physics, and chemistry, and these underlie all astronomical knowledge. The thread of human curiosity and human thinking runs through all our knowledge and should unify it.

About Mathematics

None of the elementary astronomy described just now could possibly have been developed without mathematics. We know we can count, use symbols to represent numbers, and that not only can we add, subtract, multiply, divide, etc., using procedures that everyone will recognize as valid, but also when we do, we find the numbers are consistent within themselves and the manipulations lead to no self-contradictions or conclusions that appear to be untrue. We know also that mathematicians can use logarithms to facilitate calculations without vitiating their results. We know that experts in the field of mathematics use many complex devices in their manipulations and that, regardless of cultural differences in other fields, mathematicians everywhere have little or no difficulty in agreeing with each other on fundamentals. This vast store of mathematical knowledge, accumulated over centuries, is a part of the treasury of accumulated non-controversial knowledge which the human race possesses.

About Physics and Chemistry

Physics often deals with forces and movement of material objects and seeks to understand them. In this connection it is the forerunner of technology, or engineering, which is concerned with making machines work. Newton's laws are basic: a body at rest remains at rest until some force moves it; a body in motion at uniform speed continues to move in a straight line at this speed until something diverts or stops it. These laws hold not only for heavenly bodies controlled by gravitational forces but also for all other material objects. The earth spins on its axis and will continue to do so indefinitely until something, like friction, slows it down or stops it.

We human beings have material bodies and the laws of motion apply to these. When we walk or run we continually fall forward under the influence of gravity, but we catch ourselves with each succeeding step. We, like other objects, cannot make sharp turns at high speed and, after being at rest in our beds, we cannot get moving in the morning without putting forth some effort. Because physics enters into our lives at every turn, and even when we don't turn, we need to know something about it. We can learn from sad experience not to step on a sloping ice-sheet, but if we learn from elementary physics about gravity, motion, and friction (or the lack of it), we can learn the same lesson and omit the sad experience.

We need to avoid superficiality because in physics, as well as in other sciences, things are not always what they seem. Have you ever thought, "Wouldn't it be fun to be a space traveler?" It may not seem to be so, but you and I *are* space travelers. If we regard the sun as a fixed point in the universe, we regularly travel about 1.6 million miles a day in space, riding on the surface of the earth. Even if the earth did not circle around the sun, merely by remaining stationary on the equator we would be traveling at the rate of over 1,000 miles per hour because of the spinning action of the earth. This movement, however, is almost inconsequential compared with the space travel involved in circling the sun. At this instant, again assuming the sun to be a fixed point in the universe, we are cruising along at about 67,000 miles per hour. But, in addition, if our sun with its solar system is circling around in the universe, as astronomical evidence indicates, the speed at which this is happening must also enter into our calculations. We do not *seem* to be traveling at the speed we are going because the houses we live in, the streets, trees, rivers, and lakes in our neighborhood are all traveling with us at the same speed.

Physicists know that light travels in straight lines but also that it bounces off reflective surfaces and becomes diffuse. Lenses can change the direction of a light path and this made microscopes and the early telescopes possible. Light's speed of travel is about 186,000 miles per second, and we may regard it either as a wave motion or as a stream of particles (photons). In addition to visible light, physicists know that there are many similar radiations which we do not see—infrared, ultraviolet, x-rays, radio-waves. They travel at the same speed as light and their wavelengths vary from perhaps as low as one ten-trillionth of a meter up to 20,000 meters. Light that is visible to us has wavelengths from about 0.4 microns up to about 0.8 microns (a micron is one millionth of a meter). The existence of these various radiations makes medical x-rays, radio, television, and satellite communication possible, and their existence greatly enriches astronomy by making it possible to study stellar radiations which we cannot see.

About the beginning of the 20th century physicists discovered electrons, which are extremely mobile, negatively charged particles. We know that electricity flowing through a wire is a stream of these particles. Electric currents and magnetism are closely related. Moving a wire in a magnetic field produces an electric current in the wire. We also know how to build motors which operate in response to a flow of electrons. Ordinary household electric currents are, however, something different. Instead of being a steady flow of electrons in one direction, they are alternating currents in which direction of flow commonly changes 120 times a second. This alternating back and forth flow of electrons, when passing through a fine filament, may generate light just as would a steady, one-directional flow. This alternating flow of electrons in a heating element (in an electric iron, for example) generates heat, just as a steady one-directional flow of electrons would. Our ability to generate and manipulate electron flows, etc., enters into technology in a thousand ways.

Radioactivity was discovered in the 19th century and involves the spontaneous disintegration of certain atoms (radium and others). The emission of particles and radiation and the release of energy accompany this disintegration. The harnessing of the energy contained within atoms is a 20th-century development and is the result of high-powered research. We must continue this research until we can make this energy release safe and efficient.

Electrons and other charged particles enter into the structure of atoms and thus enter into chemistry too. Copper atoms, for example, are neutral electrically, but with the removal of one or two electrons (de-electronization) they become cuprous ions, Cu^+, or cupric ions, Cu^{++}. In such a case, de-electronization is synonymous with oxidation, a common chemical process.

Chemists, like physicists, deal with material objects, but with a different approach. Their interest is in burning and similar processes in which substances undergo profound changes when they react with each other, but without any change in total weight. Such a process is the combination of hydrogen, a gas which liquefies at about -253^0C, and oxygen, a gas which liquefies at -183^0C, to produce gaseous water, which liquefies at a far higher temperature—$+100^0C$. The weight of the water which a given amount of hydrogen and oxygen produces is measurably the same as the combined weights of the hydrogen and oxygen that produced it.

Another illustration: when we heat mercury, a silver-white liquid metal, with oxygen, a colorless gas, we obtain a solid red powder. The red powder weighs the same as the mercury plus the oxygen with which the mercury has combined,

Likewise, when a stick of dynamite explodes, the amount of matter in the vicinity is the same as it was before the explosion. When a house burns to the ground the resulting ashes plus the smoke, carbon dioxide, etc., weigh the same as the house plus the oxygen used up in the burning.

The approach of chemists to material objects emphasizes the difference between "chemical substances" and mixtures.

Chemical substances are of two kinds: elementary substances which contain only one element—such as oxygen, sulfur, or iron; and compound substances which contain at least two and often many more elements. In either case, however, a substance has the same makeup throughout—analyzing one bit of a sample yields the same results as analyzing the whole.

"Mixtures," in contrast to "substances," are not uniform throughout, and we can often separate them into their constituent substances. A loaf of bread is a typical mixture and consists of starch, minerals, proteins, and other substances all mixed together. Air is a mixture of nitrogen, oxygen, and other gases which chemists can separate one from another.

Chemists know that every chemical substance consists of tiny molecules, and that if it is a pure substance the molecules are all the same. They even know how many molecules are present in any known weight of a chemical substance. Chemists often talk about and graphically represent single molecules, but typically they do not deal with them in the laboratory; usually, in the material they work with there are many millions of molecules, but in a pure chemical substance these molecules are all alike.

The most remarkable achievement of chemists is the attainment of the knowledge of the exact structure of thousands of differing molecules of different substances—how the atoms within the molecules link together and their exact geometrical pattern. Chemists can demonstrate their knowledge on this point by building molecular structures to pre-determined specifications with certainty.

One of the things which all chemists know about is catalysis. For example, when they mix hydrogen and oxygen together at ordinary temperature, the two gases do not react, but in the presence of a suitable catalyst they do. The most common catalysts and the most diversified ones are enzymes. Living cells produce these, and they occur in all the tissues of living things and promote a host of specific reactions, each enzyme performing a unique function. We could not live, and the metabolism in our bodies could not take place, without their presence. This is one of the many ways in which chemistry ties in with biology.

Thermodynamics is of about equal interest to physicists and chemists. *Thermo* refers to heat and energy and *dynamics* relates to the movement of material things, including molecules. Thermodynamics thus has to do with the relations between the two, and these relations enter into both physics and chemistry. Thermodynamics is also of interest to biologists because, if they are true scientists, they are curious, for example, about questions like why and how does a grasshopper hop; there is plenty of energy and movement involved in this process, and we cannot study it thoroughly without getting into thermodynamics.

Included in our knowledge about molecular structure is the fact that some molecules (asymmetric ones) are geometrically capable of existing in "right-handed" and "left-handed" forms. These abound in nature. The amino acids, for example, which are the building stones in protein structures, are, for the most part, asymmetric and have "left-handed" configurations. A protein built from "right-handed" amino acids would be indigestible and completely useless to our bodies. This fact ties in with the phenomena of enzyme action. Enzymes, in exhibiting catalytic activity, "know the difference" between "right-handed" and "left-handed" molecules, and the enzymes in our bodies are unable to deal with "right-handed" amino acids or proteins built from them. We occasionally find "right-handed" amino acids in nature, but the dominance of "left-handed" amino acids in all proteins, regardless of what organism gives rise to them, is a striking fact. Chemists know how to deal with "right-handed" and "left-handed" molecules of many sorts, how to distinguish between them, separate them, and use them appropriately. In order to do these things effectively, they must know about and utilize mathematics, physics, and biology as well as chemistry.

Unfortunately, many people, because of their lack of an elementary grasp of unified world-knowledge, have misconceptions about what chemists do and what chemicals are. They need to "unlearn" these misconceptions. In their minds, chemicals are stinking, poisonous things which are significant because they pollute the atmosphere and the earth. They do not realize that oxygen, which we need to get from the air we breathe minute by minute, is a *chemical*; so is the water which is essential to all life, and the carbon dioxide in the air which is essential for plant life. Salt is a chemical; so are sugar and starch; also cellulose, from which paper is made. All our foods are chemical in nature and so are all the foods for plants; all fertilizers are chemical in nature, and there is no such thing as a non-chemical fertilizer. Animal waste is a good fertilizer because it contains many of the chemicals that plants need.

Of course, some chemicals stink and many are poisonous, but the fragrances of flowers are also chemicals as are the flavors of fruits. In the laboratory, chemists can often produce by synthesis the chemicals which are responsible for these aromas and flavors. The foods that build us up and make life possible do so because of the *chemicals* they contain. There is no such thing as a non-chemical food.

Chemistry, like physics and mathematics, encompasses every material thing on earth.

About Biology—Plants, Animals, and Other Organisms

Biology is the study of living things, and everyone should know
something about it in order to understand themselves, because we
human beings are all biological specimens.

There are something like a million different kinds of organisms on
earth—plants, animals, bacteria, etc. Some of these, like bacteria and
yeast, are single-celled organisms, but the vast majority of organisms
are multicellular, and each contains numerous kinds of specialized
cells.

The insects constitute a very large group. Of all the existing known
species, the majority are insects.

The developmental history of insects is most interesting and
remarkable. For example, immediately after hatching from a fertilized egg, a butterfly is a worm (catterpiller). It then passes through a
pupal stage and eventually emerges as the familiar adult butterfly.
Chemistry and physics enter into this development in a striking way,
and a caterpillar can never become a pupa or an adult butterfly unless
it gets from its environment (by way of the food it eats) a large
assortment of specific chemical compounds which include minerals,
amino acids, and vitamins. Each of these chemicals is absolutely
essential, and if any one is missing or is in short supply, development
cannot take place in a normal fashion. The requirement for proper
food on the part of a caterpillar illustrates a universal principle of
biology: every organism, regardless of whether it is single-celled,
multicellular, plant, animal, or bacterial in nature, has to have a
suitable chemical environment which provides it with its chemical
essentials, and vital chemical exchanges always take place between
each organism and its environment.

This principle is evident in the closely related economic fact of
nature—namely, that nature does not provide automatically an
abundant, plenteous environment to any species for its support. For
example, if we provided the cells in a small cake of yeast with an
excellent, nutritious environment continuously for one week, the
mass of cells at the end of this time would weigh over a billion tons! If
it were possible to give a single cell of an intestinal bacterium, *E. coli*,
a continuous supply of *excellent* food for itself and its progeny, it

would be capable of producing a bacterial slime covering the earth one mile deep in about three days. In nature no bacterium or yeast gets this kind of pampering. The same economic principle holds for all organisms, including human beings. No species or individual organism should expect a rose-garden existence.

The developmental history of a fowl or mammal is different from that of an insect, but nonetheless astounding. Animals, besides having an instinct to procure and eat good food, also have a dominant desire to reproduce. Following this instinct, male and female animals join together; the male impregnates the female and she eventually produces young.

The same principles we have mentioned before regarding food supply apply in mammalian reproduction. For instance, a fertilized human egg cell is poised to develop embryonically into a baby, but this cannot happen unless it can obtain a wide assortment of essential chemical substances. It is a remarkable example of the unity of nature that the majority of these essential chemicals are exactly the same essential chemicals that a caterpillar needs in order to become a butterfly. In human reproduction this assortment comes by way of the food the expectant mother consumes, and the developing embryo receives it through the bloodstream. If the mother's food is deficient in any of the essential chemicals, either a miscarriage may take place or the growing embryo may be deformed. Many troubles which come to children and adults may have their roots in poorly balanced prenatal nutrition.

We call attention here to the fact that the need for ample, well-rounded nutrition exists not only prenatally but also through infancy, childhood, adolescence, and adulthood. This fact, as well as its implications for health, is one that we have not digested well nor adequately appreciated up to the present time. As a result, vast numbers of educated people have inadequate knowledge about the chemistry of nutrition and how to avoid the ills which may result from too little attention to its adequacy. In short, they do not know how to nourish and take care of their bodies.

Human genetics (heredity) is a very valuable line of study. For one thing, it helps us understand genetic diseases, of which there are many. One of its chief values, in my opinion, lies in the fact that it helps us to understand people better. To the best of my knowledge, no one has ever approached human genetics with this objective dominantly in mind.

In fowls, the vital instinct for reproduction results in sexual contact and the furnishing by the male of sperm cells capable of fertilizing egg cells. After this fertilization takes place the female fowl constructs within her body what we commonly call an egg, which she lays. This egg is far more than a fertilized egg cell; in addition, it usually contains an ample and excellent supply of the essential chemicals which the growing embryo needs during the hatching period. If the diet of the female fowl contains a deficient supply of these essential chemicals, the eggs cannot furnish the best assortment to the growing embryo and reproduction may fail. The incubation of a fertilized hen's egg presents in readily observable form one of nature's striking miracles. At the start of incubation, breaking the egg shell may result in a gooey mess. After twenty-one days of incubation, however, when the egg shell breaks, out steps a fully developed, attractive baby chick. Scientists have studied extensively the intermediate steps between the fertilized egg before incubation and the baby chick, and similar events in other species. This type of study constitutes the field of science known as embryology.

In line with the unity of nature, there are many resemblances between the embryologies and the developmental histories of different species. For example, the very same *nucleotides* (containing combined phosphoric acid, a sugar with five carbon atoms, and a pyrimidine or purine base) enter into the process of heredity in every kind of organism whether unicellular or multicellular, and an assortment of these nucleotides constitutes a code, or blueprint, for the proteins and other chemical structures which are built as development proceeds. We have already mentioned the unity with respect to the dominance of "left-handed" amino acids in all proteins. We have also mentioned the unity which encompasses the fact that the very same amino acids and B-vitamins, for example, enter into the make-up of the metabolic machinery of such diverse organisms as caterpillars and human beings and the unifying fact that all organisms utilize enzymes to promote metabolism.

Nature exhibits its unity in another most peculiar way. For instance, within each species of plant and animal individuality exists.

In other words, each individual organism is, at least to a degree, unique. In many cases this uniqueness is merely interesting—like the fact that every snowflake in a snowstorm may exhibit a distinctive pattern. But in other cases, such as the individuality which human beings exhibit, the uniqueness is not merely interesting, it is crucial. If human beings were strictly carbon copies of each other, living in the world together would be an entirely different situation from that which exists in the real world today.

We have known at least since 1926 that mammals, of which human beings are examples, often exhibit a vast degree of individuality. At that time Wade Brown of the Rockefeller Institute dissected 645 male rabbits, determined their organ weights, and found that these organ weights (when he corrected for differences in body size) varied from two- to eighty-fold and that not only the average but also the median variation was about ten-fold. Likewise, as we have noted on p.31, with the publication of Barry Anson's *3 Atlas of Human Anatomy* in 1951, it became evident that human variations in anatomy are often striking and probably significant, although Dr. Anson did not discuss this significance.

From the human viewpoint, the fact that every human being exhibits striking uniqueness—anatomically, neurologically, endocrinologically, metabolically, and in the structure of his or her brain, digestive tract, respiratory tract, circulatory system, etc.—is a most momentous one and one with which every educated person must be acquainted. If one leaves this fact out of biology it is indeed a sad and inexcusable omission.

The field of biology exemplifies some of the most striking and interesting facts in mathematics, physics, and chemistry. I was greatly impressed many years ago, as an undergraduate studying mathematics, when we proved, in effect, by the use of calculus, that hexagonal cylinders packed together were the most economical storage bins with respect to the amount of building material used. Triangular or square or circular cylinders would be far less economical. Our professor noted that bees and other insects have "known" these facts and have used hexagonal cylinders in their honeycombs and nests for millennia.

We find in the field of biology some of the most interesting phenomena of physics in the electrical realm as exemplified by the electric eel, brain waves, and the electrical phenonena associated with other living cells. And the most remarkable and outstanding phenomenon known in the field of photochemistry is photosynthesis, the lack of which would abolish or overturn the whole biological world economy. We can find by far the most intriguing and intricate examples of chemical catalysis in the enzymes which are basic to all metabolism in the entire biological realm.

From this knowledge of biology it is clear that there is a tremendous unity in all of nature and that mathematics, physics, chemistry, and biology are all closely knit together.

About Geology

Geology is in part biology. Geologists learn how to trace the history of life on earth through the study of the fossil remains in various strata. They have learned how to tell the relative age of rocks from their location in the stratifications; they also use radioactive dating (physics and chemistry). Paleontologists have found that in the young rocks fossil remains of complex forms of life exist, but that in the more ancient rocks the fossil remains of only simpler organisms exist. Extensive studies in this area have led to the general belief that more complex forms of life have *evolved* from simpler ones. Most students of biology are sure that evolution has taken place, but of course there is haziness with respect to many details. Those who believe that man originated by a special creation, of course, reject the idea of general evolution.

By tracing the movements of land masses (even continents), geologists have gained much insight into earthquakes and volcanoes.

The facts of geology relate closely to those of mathematics, physics, chemistry, biology, archeology, climatology, and geography. Geology is thus clearly a unifying science.

About People

People the world over are basically alike. They differ from all other organisms in their thinking and in the fact that they have complex languages with which they express their thoughts. However, there is diversity too. They have different body builds (physiques) and differ

in size, hair growth, hair color, skin color, and eye color. Some
(particularly men) have a substantial growth of hair on their bodies,
while others have very little. In some, the hair texture is kinky in
nature; in others it is extremely straight; in still others it is intermediate. Hair colors vary from deep black to blond, and eyes from light
blue to very dark brown.

We have already noted (p. 31) that people are always unique
individuals. Each one has his or her own peculiarities; these are
basically anatomical and biochemical but doubtless carry over into
psychology as well.

Biology tells us, if we will listen, that every inbred population of
human beings is bound to be, to a degree, distinctive. These peculiarities may be in anatomy, endocrinology, neurology, psychology, etc.
While they may be trivial, there is no guarantee whatever that they
are. Our specific knowledge with respect to differences between the
"races" or "ethnic groups" is very meager indeed. In fact, the terms
"race" and "ethnic groups" are loose ones, and we have great difficulty even in defining them. It is not fashionable (to put it mildly) for
scientists to devote themselves to investigations of this sort. Extensive
experiments with animals, however, have convinced me that it is
highly important for us to understand these differences. By careful
study it is possible to distinguish between populations of experimental animals coming from different breeding stocks even though they
supposedly are of the same species and have similar genetic
backgrounds.

There are a number of gaps in our knowledge which we must fill in
before we can have a truly comprehensive knowledge about people.
One has to do with the innate differences (particularly psychological)
between men and women. Another concerns the differences between
ethnic groups. It would be of tremendous advantage in our human
relations if we had dependable knowledge in these two areas.

If we had this knowledge we would still recognize that individuals
are unique. People are extremely complex, with dozens of facets to
their lives, and this makes it impossible to classify them in any simple
way. Superficial talk about certain races being generally superior and
others being generally inferior (as was prevalent during the Nazi
regime) is intolerable because people are *unique individuals*; they do
not fall within recognizable distinctive patterns.

One of the best available ways of gaining understanding of people is to read biographies, especially if they are penetrating and do not deal with superficialities. The assortment of biographies available in different cultures and different locations will be highly distinctive, but in every culture there have been remarkable individuals worthy of attention.

We will have more to say about people in the next section under the heading of Psychology.

About Psychology

Psychology is a most important part of biology, and it becomes more and more important as we consider the higher forms of life.

Psychology is fundamentally "the science of the mind" (according to Webster's Unabridged Dictionary). Since minds are intangible entities and thus difficult to study and explore, many psychologists prefer an easier task—that of studying behavior—and they would change the definition of psychology accordingly. But I believe a consensus will grant that the mind is something very real and worthy of study, provided we can find a way to do it.

What we *know* about psychology would fill a much smaller book than what we surmise about it. We know, for example, that we have within our craniums a large mass of nerve tissue—the brain—and that there are numerous nerves that carry messages to and from it. Everyone agrees that the messages coming to the brain from the sense organs are impulses of a dot-and-dash variety and that the brain must interpret these impulses in order that we may perceive their meaning. For example, when our two retinas receive slightly different images simultaneously, the individual retinal cells send separate impulses to the brain. The brain interprets these numerous messages not to signify the existence of two slightly different outside worlds but that of one world in three-dimensional space. The various sense organs— the eyes, the ears, the nerve endings in the skin which register pressure, temperatures, and pain, the olfactory nerves, the taste buds—by themselves cannot perform usefully. We involve our interpretative brain whenever we perceive anything.

The most important thing that our minds do is to think. This is an area about which we *know* little. We do not know how we think or what motivates us to think, but no one would argue with the fact that life without thinking would be blank and meaningless.

We know that when we behave in a certain way and accompany or reinforce this with pleasurable sensations, we are much more likely to repeat the behavior.

We know many interesting things about intelligence. We can measure it imperfectly and, thanks to psychologists, including L.L. Thurston of the University of Chicago, we know that intelligence does not come in a single bundle but that it consists of *primary abilities* that are largely independent of each other. Thurston brought biology into psychology by recognizing that these *primary abilities* are innate and arise from heredity. Arithmetical facility, word familiarity, rote memory, and spatial imagery were among the *primary abilities* which he recognized. A person may be very able with respect to arithmetic but weak in word familiarity and vice versa. As a matter of fact, everyone's mental pattern tends to be spotted, and being able in one particular area carries no guarantee whatever that the person will be able in another area. The fact that sometimes "freakish" youngsters are severely retarded mentally in some ways and yet are extraordinarily able in others dramatically shows us that intelligence is not unitary in nature. Such individuals include those who have outstanding ability in art or music or arithmetic or rote memory and who can perform remarkable feats in the particular field in which they have a special ability.

We can best appreciate the fact that "non-freakish" individuals also have unique patterns of mind and personality and look at the world in entirely different ways when we read intimate biographies and recognize the unique contributions and predilections of notable individuals. Thoughtful reading of any group of intimate biographies shows that uniqueness of mind is the rule, not the exception. We learn without effort not to expect Shakespeare to be an Einstein or Einstein to be a Shakespeare. We recognize full well that Abraham Lincoln was not an Edison, neither was Edison an Abraham Lincoln. It is very clear to us that Leonardo da Vinci was not a Wolfgang Amadeus Mozart and that Mozart was not a Napoleon nor a Benjamin Franklin nor a Benvenuto Cellini.

One of the most deep-seated benefits we obtain from studying psychology is that we learn better *what people are like*. If we recognize that they are "spotted" in their minds as well as in their tastes and inclinations, we have learned a great deal about them. If we do not learn this from our psychological and biological study, we might as well throw these sciences out the window. People have distinctive human minds, and there are many qualities which these minds possess. If we do not recognize that minds are distinctive we are missing most of the show. As we have emphasized, one of the prime prerequisites for living in this world is to understand the people who are our fellow inhabitants.

People are always curious mixtures. Everyone has, innately, a selfish streak in his or her nature because self-preservation is the first law of life. While we need to recognize this selfishness in everyone, this does not mean the absence of altruism. There certainly is no rule of law or biology which says that a person must be consistent within himself or herself. If there were such a rule, we would all be in violation of it. For instance, we could never be both stingy and generous, but most of us are. Nothing has done more to impede progress in understanding our fellow humans than the convictions that the hypothetical "average man" and "average woman" should be the center of scientific attention and that distinctiveness is trivial.

There are several practical things we learn from psychology in addition to the fact that everybody is an individual and needs to be recognized as such. One of these is the fact that while men's and women's minds tend to be different from each other, they are not as different as has commonly been supposed. While as a rule it is true that women are less inclined to be mechanical than men, there are some women who excel in mechanics. In every special activity—law, medicine, ministry, science, engineering, politics, business, art, and music—women can successfully compete with men. This is a profoundly important fact that people in general are just beginning to accept and digest.

Another insight we gain from psychology is that the direct "pursuit of happiness" is often futile. A person who is continually looking into himself or herself and is planning and scheming above all else to be happy usually fails to attain his or her objective. A much better recipe for happiness involves working diligently at a productive job, having interests outside oneself, and trying to do things that will make others happy.

One investigator that I know of has done an experiment like this many times. He has asked a group of people first to write down the names of ten people whom they individually know most intimately, and then to rate them on the basis of how happy they think each one to be. At a later time, without reference to the "happiness" ratings, he asked them to rate these same people on the basis of their unselfishness and willingness to help others. When he gathered together and compared all these "happiness" and "unselfishness" ratings with respect to many individuals he found with consistency that the happiest persons are those who are the most unselfish.

These experiments support the validity of the Golden Rule. This Golden Rule, in its essentials, appears in the sacred writings of many religions. In addition, Socrates, Plato, and Aristotle promulgated or echoed the same teaching. The following statements are at least worth thinking about: "When we wrong another person, we automatically wrong ourselves." "When we benefit another person we automatically benefit ourselves." These statements seem to be psychologically sound. How sweet it would be if everyone understood, believed in, and lived by these maxims!

About Economics

Let's start with what we *know* from biology. Human beings are the most advanced form of life we know about, and there is reason to think that the human species demand preservation above all others. We *know*, also from biology, that in order to preserve human life there is an absolute necessity for adequate food. If the climate demands it, people must also have shelter and clothing. They also may *want* many other things—education, escape from drudgery, beautiful homes and gardens, transportation, amusements, security, privacy, etc. An individual's economic status is satisfactory if he or she is able to satisfy all his or her needs and a reasonable number of his or her wants. If *families* are a part of the social scheme, the economic situation is satisfactory if they can fill all their needs and a reasonable quota of the wants of the family members. This same statement holds for cities, states, or countries.

We learn from biology that no organism should automatically expect to receive a bountiful existence that supplies it with every need and want. One of the fundamental facts in the field of economics is that every product and every service costs somebody something in the way of work or its equivalent. In general, there is no such thing as a free ride or a free lunch. Of course, a small baby nursing at its mother's breast does get a free lunch, and small children are commonly provided for by their parents. But in the adult world it is different, and children need to learn to make this transition early by making contributions of their own. The general principle of "something for nothing" doesn't work; in economics, somebody has to pay. Life is, and should be, a struggle for betterment.

How should we organize ourselves in order to gain the economic ends on which we may all agree? The answer to this question is *we do not know*, and there is room for differences of opinion. In some countries people accept kings, queens, emperors, or czars to rule over them, and in some cases this has seemed to work. But if we have monarchs on a hereditary basis, sooner or later the monarchs who are good-looking, benevolent, strong and charismatic produce progeny who lack these qualities. Then the monarchies may fail.

If we rule out hereditary monarchies, the question arises, "What kind of a government will be able to satisfy our economic needs and desires?" If political scientists have a foolproof answer to this question, they have not revealed it in a convincing manner. One of the fundamental problems that confronts them is this: should everyone enjoy the very same economic status? Biology tells us that this is impossible and that in many species, including *Homo sapiens*, there are natural leaders and natural followers; and furthermore, because of individuality, what satisfies some individuals would not be at all satisfying to others. We cannot abolish diversity. Even if we accept a communistic ideal, we find that in practice some are leaders and some are not.

Most countries of the world need to experiment and explore continuously to find out how they can best organize their society in order to attain the economic and other goals they cherish. With respect to what these goals are, most people of the world are not far from agreement. With respect to how to attain these goals, however, people are far from agreement, partly because of a lack of unified world-knowledge, coordinated education, and means of effective communication.

We must solve the problems of taxation, defense, and economic fair play on the basis of unified knowledge in the various fields involved.

About Ethics

Our society regards a retarded person who does not know right from wrong as unfit to stand trial (The M'Naghten Rule), so some moral sense is universal among "normal" people. The possession of moral sense *seems to be* the exclusive possession of human beings in contrast to lower animals. It is interesting that a philosopher has recently taken the position that the more enlightened a person is, the more trustworthy is his conscience (see page 116). This sounds reasonable. A small baby presumably has no conscience at all, but develops one as he or she becomes more knowledgeable. Since millions of people have a moral sense and measure their conduct by this sense, ethics is something which should deeply concern us all. It is a part of life. While it would be difficult to extemporize a non-controversial code of ethics that almost everyone would accept, there is a widespread sense of moral values upon which many diverse people agree.

If citizens of one country were to accuse nationals from another country of lying, stealing, cheating, torturing, and killing, it would be most unlikely that they would respond to the accusation by saying, "Such acts as these are in accord with the ethical principles we follow and are justifiable." The defense of the accused would likely be, "We did not commit those acts." Most literate people recognize that lying, cheating, stealing, torturing, and killing are reprehensible. There is much unity among peoples with respect to ethical principles.

About the Unseen

Two facts stand out even though they may seem extremely strange: 1) we encounter many all-important unseen non-material "things" in life; 2) it is these unseen "things" that make the earth, sun, moon, stars, mathematics, physics, chemistry, biology, geology, people, psychology, economics, and ethics what they are. These "things" unify all knowledge.

Among these "things" are, first, mathematical principles. These are difficult to delineate, but we can clarify them by a few examples. If we have four apples and take away two, two are left. The principle is the same and holds true whether we are dealing with apples, bananas, coconuts, or anything else.

When "the farmer takes a wife," this is (among other things) a mathematical event; there are now two mouths to feed and two for whom they must provide shelter. If there are eight children born to them, there are now ten mouths to feed and ten bodies to shelter. The Chinese have a very practical mathematical problem; they realize that they cannot tolerate over-population. Their mathematical solution is this: encourage couples to have not more than one child.

The matter of simple arithemetic is something we recognize as being infallible; we do not argue about it or try to modify it but accept it as irrevocable truth. If we have to travel 100 miles and our vehicle can go only 20 miles per hour, there is absolutely no way we can arrive at our destination in less than five hours.

We know that the circumference of a circle is about 3.1416 times the diameter, and it doesn't make any difference whether the circle is the size of a pinhead or has the diameter of 8,000 miles. Likewise, the sum of the angles of a triangle expressed in degrees is 180°, regardless of the size or shape of the triangle. It doesn't matter how we measure these angles, the more accurately we do so the closer the sum adds up the 180°!

Such principles as these mathematical ones we cannot change or modify. They are unseen, eternal truths which our minds accept, and we adjust our lives to them.

Besides mathematical principles we also encounter physical laws and principles—the laws of gravitation, motion, and those involving energy and electricity—which are unseen but which are basic to day and night, the wind and the weather, and the seasons. They also impinge on everything we do.

We must adjust to the laws of motion; for example, if we do so we never will travel at high speed without having facilities to stop gracefully without a smash-up. If we have the proper regard for electricity and lightning we will not stand under a lone, tall tree during a rainstorm, nor will we burn our homes down by improperly wiring them. There is no escape from these principles. We cannot take the

Fifth Amendment. It would be silly to criticize water for running downhill or to argue with or complain about the laws of gravity and motion. This would be like "arguing with God."

We also encounter in life the intricate laws of chemistry which we must also accept. There are certain chemical substances which, when we take them into our bodies, will cause us pain, distress, and even death. There are other chemical substances which, by their nature, act beneficently; they give us energy and strength and promote health. There are, in fact, more than forty chemicals which are indispensable and without which we cannot continue to live.

The principles which govern all these chemical actions, whether constructive or destructive, are invisible and untouchable, yet we cannot live without them.

Nature's laws in every possible realm are unseen influences which help make our lives what they are.

If one thinks about it for a few moments one realizes that love, for example, is an unseen influence quite apart from the items which we have been discussing and that there are many other unseen influences in our lives. Among these are friendships, comradeship, and the sense of belonging to a group. An outstanding "incompleteness" in our whole educational system is the fact that we do not recognize these as unseen factors or develop an appreciation of their deeper meaning. This confuses our whole education. We need to recognize continuously and remember all these unseen principles and forces because they are always with us and influence us from infancy throughout life. Perhaps the mathematical principles, etc., which we have discussed are the tip of the iceberg or perhaps the tips of several icebergs.

We often take for granted that our homes will contain "home furnishings" such as chairs, tables, carpets, beds, pictures, TV sets, etc. We should not overlook the desirability of having unseen "home furnishings" such as the spirit of patience, hope, responsibility, cheerfulness, goodwill, and love, coupled with the avoidance of the spirit of frustration, despair, and hatred. The unseen "home furnishings" make more difference than the chairs or carpets; unseen things in life are far from trivialities and call for serious attention in our education.

With an appreciation of the unseen, we can then place the other factors of life in proper perspective. Does it not seem obvious that if we plan and live our lives on the assumption that love, hope, aspirations, and moral sense do exist and do count, we are building our lives on a sound foundation with proper perspective?

All the items in the above Compendium are related one to another and flow as in a single stream. There is certainly nothing final about this Compendium as I have written it. As I have noted earlier it is subject to improvement and expansion. It is a start, however, and points the way toward something even better.

Chapter VII

One Major Way We Can Help Knit the Peoples of the Earth Together

I believe my readers will agree that it will be highly desirable if the peoples of the world from different cultures can meet on common ground and discuss problems, disagreeing if necessary without, however, being disagreeable. I see how we can accomplish this in a simple, direct, practical way by using diplomacy and carefully cultivating goodwill, recognizing people as they really are. The *common ground* is a crucial part of my proposal. Following the strategy I suggest will bring marvelous benefits even if at first it is not completely successful.

Someone has expressed one of the fundamental concepts of practical psychology in this way: "Do not start a negotiation with a person who may turn out to be an adversary by poking your finger in his eye." If we are to draw peoples of the world of different cultures together, we had best start with trying to find out what it is, if anything, upon which they might immediately agree. Certainly it will not be on sectarian religion, politics, or economics. There is hope, however, that they may find common ground in non-controversial world-knowledge.

One plan would be to induce leaders from various diverse cultures to do what I have attempted to do in the previous chapter—set forth in a simple way what they think to be the body of *non-controversial* knowledge that people in general should have. All of this material from different cultures would be most interesting and illuminating. If people from different cultures can become genuinely curious and considerate of what people in other cultures think to be mandatory knowledge, this in itself will be a giant step forward and will help bring people together. In addition the amount of fundamental agreement might surprise us. We could probably make a synthesis (sticking to the non-controversial) which would, after multilingual negotiation, be generally acceptable. All of the negotiators involved in this formulation would gain invaluable information and insight by considering what people from different cultures think to be non-controversial and what they think to be indispensable knowledge. Such discussions would contribute greatly to the education of everyone who had the privilege to participate.

If we are to accomplish this, it is essential that we emphasize the importance of what we feel we *know* in contrast to what we may surmise, conjecture, or express as mere opinion. This body of knowledge, about which we feel certain, would be an excellent starting point from which we could evolve serious discussions of subjects which would have previously led to disruption and dissatisfaction.

The fact that in many specific areas the best minds in the world are already completely compatible and have no difficulty in finding common agreement greatly supports the idea that *we can cultivate understanding*. For example, mathematicians all over the world use the same symbolism, speak the same language of mathematics, and have no difficulty agreeing with each other on all fundamentals. It is obvious in this area that human minds think along certain lines and the ideas which appeal to some often find unanimous and enthusiastic approval.

One of the reasons this concordance exists in the field of mathematics is that mathematicians deal with things about which they are *certain* and do not traffic in opinions, surmises, and conjectures.

The same concordance of the best minds is noted also in the field of physics. There is no such thing as Swedish physics, Italian physics, or Soviet physics. All physicists the world over tend to agree on the fundamentals. The basic principles are the same everywhere.

In the wide field of chemistry there is also a profound unity of thought. The international atomic weights, for example, are truly international; no country or culture is tempted to say, "We want a set of atomic weights all our own." All chemists recognize that an element (or isotope) which has a specific atomic weight has the same atomic weight wherever it exists. There is no provincialism in this regard. Any chemist in any country, if he wishes to do so, can re-determine any atomic weight, and if he provides convincing evidence that a specific atomic weight is slightly in error, chemists the world over will accept the change in this value. There are no secrets with respect to how atomic weights are determined.

Again, one of the reasons why chemists all over the world agree is because they deal with *certainties*, not with surmises. For example, the fundamental structural makeup of quinine is well established and there is no tendency to argue about it. The same is true of thousands of other complex substances.

There is such a thing as a "world astronomy" and astronomers the world over accept the same basic facts. Astronomers in one country routinely disseminate their findings to those in other countries. Those countries which have few telescopes and poor astronomical equipment do not have any need to set up an astronomical science of their own.

In the fields of mathematics, physics, chemistry, and astronomy we may say with confidence that knowledge is unified and that learned persons in all these fields find the widest agreement. We cannot say, however, that all knowledge is unified. There are branches of knowledge like sociology, economics, and political science in which the certainties are relatively few and the surmises and conjectures are relatively plentiful. When we get into these fields

88 RETHINKING EDUCATION

there is likely to be dispute and controversy. When certainties are dominant over surmises and we have coordinated the different areas of knowledge with each other, we will greatly enhance the chances of general agreement.

Human minds, broadly speaking, do think alike, and there is a high degree of unity in mathematics, physics, chemistry, and astronomy; there is no good reason why we cannot extend this unity to all fields of knowledge wherever we can recognize non-controversial knowledge. As soon as we have a substantial body of non-controversial knowledge in the fields of psychology, economics, social science, and political science, we can expect to find essential unity in the thinking of all peoples in these fields. Social scientists and psychologists, therefore, have a mandate to strengthen their disciplines and to cultivate and coordinate the various branches of social science so that they can deal far more with certainties and far less with surmises.

Education is a powerful tool, the potency of which we can hardly exaggerate. If the educational content is non-controversial and makes sense to those who receive the education, it is doubly powerful.

Disagreements between people often arise because their thinking is based upon different foundations. Many such disagreements will largely disappear when people have sound knowledge as the basis for their education.

Complete uniformity in all cultures would be unthinkable. People in different cultures are certain to have different aptitudes, customs, tastes, likes, and dislikes; these add charm to life and should not be lost. However, people of different cultures can be drawn together emotionally with more effectiveness if their education is based upon a common core of knowledge. Diverse tastes, opinions, surmises, and speculations with respect to literature, poetry, music, art, sculpture, etc., need not conflict in any way with the single core of basic knowledge.

When we build our education on this solid core, disseminate it widely and more fully develop unified world-knowledge, we will knit the peoples of the world together in a way that is quite impossible when education is disorderly.

If we can build a satisfactory, coordinated Compendium of non-controversial knowledge and incorporate it, *in substance*, into the education of every youngster in every culture, we will have gone a long way toward bringing unity to the human race.

Chapter VIII

Human Understanding, Human Values, Human Valuables

In the previous chapter we have indicated that we can establish a sound basis for friendship among the peoples of the world if those in each culture know what they and their neighbors regard as the most indispensable knowledge.

But this is not enough. People in different cultures need to know what makes their neighbors tick, what they value most highly in life, what is most annoying, and many other things.

We are now ready to consider in more detail and more pointedly the most damning indictment of our whole educational system (to me it is unanswerable): we never learn in schools and colleges, or seek coherently to learn, the most vital lesson of all—*to understand*

90

ourselves and our fellow humans. We cannot possibly understand ourselves or learn how to take care of ourselves intelligently unless we recognize, by interdisciplinary study, that every person is a unique individual. We cannot learn this or many other vital facts about human nature on the basis of the work of a series of specialists, each confined to his or her own watertight scientific compartment. Since human beings are exceedingly complex in makeup, we can understand them only by employing a comprehensive approach which encompasses their anatomy, physiology, biochemistry, endocrinology, psychology, emotions, aspirations, and everything else that enters into their being.

In my book *The Human Frontier* (Harcourt Brace, 1946), I evidenced an awareness of this unfortunate situation, one which has changed but little in the intervening thirty-nine years. I wrote, "*Human beings* enter into every social problem, they are to a considerable extent unknowns, and one of the basic problems of social sciences is to make human beings better known—to find out as completely as may be possible how and why they behave as they do.

"The full cogency and power of this idea has never been seized upon. Certainly society has made no all-out comprehensive attempt to use the potentialities of natural science in attempting to understand human beings and their functioning in society. We have talked and written about man and have utilized an enormous tonnage of humid air and printer's ink, but in the light of its importance, our scientific investigation of human beings has been puerile in comparison with the *thoroughness* with which we have studied steel, concrete and uranium 235. . . . Man has been studied in pieces and not in his entirety, and we have been so devoted in our scientific work to the biological robot, *man-in-the-abstract*, that much of our knowledge is of very limited value from the social standpoint. Society can by no means be dealt with as though it were made up of individuals who are all alike, and yet this scientifically untenable conception is the basis of a large part of our social thinking and acting."

The scientific world knows almost nothing about the innate characteristics of human individuals or those of specific ethnic or cultural groups. This is a badly neglected field. Information about individuals could be used to study development and in many other ways. A study of these characteristics would include an appraisal of what seem to be the most important things in life. Another type of human profile would be a composite of the profiles of a population within a special group or culture. While there is a strong presumption that the *group profiles* of the Chinese, Hindus, Arabs, Israelis, Soviets, and Irish woud be distinctively different from each other, we have no scientific information on this.

A kind of profile which would be relatively easy to determine and at the same time most revealing, would be one in which specific "valuables" would be rated by different individuals and by different cultural groups. From my experience with the "Utopia Game," described in my book *You Are Extraordinary* (Random House, 1967), I know that individual profiles of this sort are profoundly different and distinctive. A "valuable" which is given a very high rating by one "normal" individual might be given a rating of zero by another. The diversity among "normal" people of similar age and education is incredibly great. As we have already indicated, differences in group profiles of this sort between different ethnic groups are totally unknown.

Following is a list of some of the human "Valuables" that I would nominate as being potentially important. These "Valuables" can be the basis for the determination of individual and group profiles.

HUMAN VALUABLES
What Is Your Profile?

1. Good health
2. A loving husband or wife
3. Babies and small children
4. Friends
5. An attractive, comfortable home
6. Security and safety
7. A garden
8. Flowers
9. Pets
10. An attractive, worthwhile job
11. Books to read
12. Shows to see
13. Newspapers, magazines
14. Music
15. Poetry
16. Literature
17. Art
18. Being well informed in science
19. Being well informed in history
20. Being well informed in

politics

21. Being well informed in athletics
22. Ability to sing beautifully
23. Competence in playing a musical instrument
24. Inventing
25. Being a forceful speaker
26. Buying and selling
27. Good looks
28. Being well groomed and dressed
29. Being admired
30. Enjoying social conversation
31. Being a good cook
32. Eating fine foods
33. Alcoholic drinks
34. Heterosexual gratification
35. Constructing things
36. Collecting things
37. Jewelry
38. Automobiles
39. Boats
40. Radio
41. Television
42. Travel
43. Hiking or other outdoor recreation
44. Watching birds and wild animals
45. Shooting birds and wild animals
46. Fishing
47. Athletic contests
48. Dancing
49. The game of chess
50. Gambling
51. Card games
52. Carnivals, circuses, etc.
53. "Being somebody"
54. Ability to lead others
55. Helping others in need
56. Craftsmanship
57. Wealth and influence
58. Fame
59. Freedom
60. Religious worship
61. Honesty and integrity
62. Patience
63. Meekness
64. Combativeness
65. Intuitiveness
66. Orderliness
67. Cleanliness
68. Gracefulness
69. Peace and serenity
70. Hope for the future
71. "Belonging" to a spouse
72. "Belonging" to a family
73. "Belonging" to a club or social group
74. "Belonging" to a political unit—neighborhood, city, state, or nation
75. "Belonging" to the human race

When profiles are determined for investigative purposes, it is recommended that the preceding list of "Valuables" be regarded as suggestive rather than definitive. Also, a suitable rating system must be devised. The list is open to amendment and improvement.

You (and your friends) can make a start at your own profile by deciding which of the above "Valuables"would compete for a position if you were selecting only five items, and which if you were selecting ten, fifteen, or twenty. These partial profiles of different individuals, when compared with each other, will demonstrate clearly how great the divergence may be among "normal" people.

To obtain a group profile, a representative selection of individuals within the group would each list the items in order of importance to them and someone would then derive from this a composite rating.

If different cultural groups can know their own group profiles and the group profiles of other cultural groups, this will be a tremendous step forward in getting the peoples of the world acquainted with each other. They will then be in a far better position to become friends.

We can extend human profiles to include metabolic profiles, psychological profiles, and profiles with respect to many different tastes—in food, music, art, literature, etc. Society has never really developed or used any comprehensive human profiles. Such profiles, if available, could help us *tremendously* to understand people better. There are many reasons, cumulative in nature, all related to my own extensive study of human individuality, which convince me that *the more we understand each other the better we will like each other.*

There are two compelling, potent reasons why understanding ourselves is so all-important:

First, if we human beings understand ourselves and each other as we really are, we will get along much better with ourselves, in our families, communities, schools, churches, synagogues, cities, states, and nations. Internationally we would not spend our time, energy or resources in killing each other off. *There is no substitute for human understanding as a means of fostering better human relations.*

Secondly, if we more fully understand ourselves we can learn to guard our health and prevent many diseases by adapting our unique, individual selves to the exceedingly complex environment in which each one of us has to live. Without a better understanding of ourselves and our potentials it will be utterly impossible to attain this goal.

There are many ways in which we are ignorant of ourselves.

Practically (that is, in individual cases) we don't know how, except in a few instances, to use hormone therapy effectively. Individually, how are your prostaglandins working? Is there anything we can do to improve their performance? What peculiarities exist in people's immune systems? Why is it that sometimes they work and sometimes they don't? Sometimes they work to our disadvantage. How important is interferon? Why is it that in humans (and guinea pigs) there appears to be a *tremendous* variation in ascorbic acid needs? Is there a spiritual aspect to every human life? Is this important? Is psychological healing possible? (Many physicians will answer this latter question, "Yes." *The New England Journal of Medicine*, for example, described in detail Norman Cousins' dramatic experience involving both laughter and vitamin C. However, because we are not fully· acquainted with ourselves, most physicians have little idea of how, in individual cases, to make psychological healing effective and useful.)

We all live in an environment that is exceedingly complex. There are thousands of kinds of chemicals that can enter into our bodies and affect us. There are thousands of inheritance factors which affect our susceptibility to disease. Can inheritance alone account for these differing susceptibilities or are environmental factors also involved? Why, in some instances, do bones heal very rapidly and sometimes very slowly? Hereditary factors are doubtless involved; are there not also important environmental factors? Why are some individuals afflicted with arthritis and others not? Are there not environmental as well as inheritance factors involved? We live in a very complex *chemical* environment, and we desperately need to know how to adjust our individual selves to it.

The human race has abundant reason for being thoroughly ashamed of itself for not having striven seriously to learn the most important lesson of all—*understanding the members of the human family.* Over 2,000 years ago Socrates wrote, in effect: "I must first know myself; to be curious about the extraneous while I am still ignorant about myself would be ridiculous." We may quote Socrates, but we have paid very little serious heed to his admonition.

This disgraceful neglect becomes more apparent when we realize that an unknown Hindu writer, one of the founders of Ayurvedic medicine, wrote in Sanskrit, reportedly about 5,000 years ago, "The individual constitution [Prakriti] is an inherited condition that cannot be altered fundamentally. It is a life-long concern for every individual. This factor of individual personality is of supreme significance in determining the conditions of health and disease in man." A highly sophisticated student of genetics and inheritance could make this statement in the 1980s and it would be just as true as it was 5,000 years ago. How blind we human beings have been to the facts and pertinency of individuality! The failure to grasp these facts introduces an absolute barrier. Without them, it is impossible to understand *anybody*, because we are *all* individuals. History is replete with instances where lack of human understanding has led to disaster.

We should not look upon the cultivation of human understanding as a "quick fix" of the ills of society. It will take time—and we must start early with children—for it to have its full effect.

However, during my forty years in the southwestern United States I have seen how, by exercising our consciences and developing a better informed public opinion, the residents of this area have adopted an incomparably more understanding attitude toward black and other minorities. Most of this took place only recently within a comparatively few years. It is clear that forces are already at work to bring us better days.

If we can introduce the spirit of unified world-knowledge into our educational system—and this will have as one of its major objectives getting acquainted with people as they really are—the results will become evident within a few years. To change the whole climate of world opinion toward a more common-sense view might not take as much time as we would think.

It would have been greatly advantageous if we human beings had begun to develop unified world-knowledge fifty, one hundred, two hundred, or more years ago, but we did not. However, if we begin now, it is basically so sound and so timely that it will probably bear substantial fruit within the lifetime of many now living.

Chapter IX

The Turn We Should Not Take

Down the road I see a fatal turn that Science must not take. In a relatively short space I can tell what this turn is and why we must avoid it and get on with more important, positive endeavors.

There are signs of this turn already in sight. Garrett Hardin (of the University of California at Santa Barbara) wrote in his book *Biology: Its Human Implications* (1949) as though science had already made this "turn" and presumably most scientists accepted it. His wording was (p. 21), "At the outset, it is necessary to appreciate the self-imposed limitations of Science. It deals only with material things, with things that can be reported on in an objective fashion, things that can be seen, heard, felt, tasted, or smelled, and with no others."

With all due respect to my colleague, this statement is simply not so. Time is not a material thing, yet Science deals with it consistently. Space is not material, yet Science deals with this whenever occasion demands it. Numbers are not material things, but of course scientists use them most appropriately. We can make *symbols* for numbers out of any material we wish, and of any weight and size we desire, but the numbers that the symbols stand for are *ideas* and, like other ideas, they have no material existence. I believe most mathematicians agree that the number 6, for example, has no specific size, does not occupy space, and weighs nothing. We deal with numbers in our minds, and indeed there is an important "science of numbers."

There are two kinds of entities which exist in the world around us and influence our lives. There are material things which we all recognize, but there are also non-material intangibles—mathematical principles, physical principles, chemical principles, etc., which are foundation stones on which our lives are built. These are just as real as are the material things.

If we restrict Science to material things which we can see, touch, and taste, this will lead us into a philosophy of determinism and irresponsibility and will banish all aspirations and idealism. This would make Science intolerable for human beings, who by nature are far more than aggregates of matter tumbling about in space.

This is a good time to remind ourselves that *science* and *knowledge* are synonymous terms and that true scientists are concerned with all knowledge, not merely with a single fragment of knowledge.

Enlightenment will ensure that we do not take this wrong turn toward materialism and determinism.

Chapter X

"Mind-Stuff" (Gedankenstoffe)—
A Major Concern; The Origin and
Development of Life

Anyone who contemplates restricting science to material things should first consider and analyze the following couplet from Robert Louis Stevenson:

The world is so full of a number of things
I'm sure we should all be as happy as kings.

What are these marvelous *things* that the poet speaks of—things that the world is so full of and that are capable of giving us so much happinesss and satisfaction that we can live life with enthusiasm? Some of these *things*, no doubt, are purely material in nature, like gold and silver, diamonds and rubies. However, a large number of the desirable *things* in life are entirely different; they belong in a completely different realm, that which the German word *Gedanken-stoffe* best defines. This German word is best translated as "mind-stuff." Mind-stuff is non-material and is something we can comprehend and handle only with our minds, like mathematical principles, laws of gravitation and motion, the laws and mini-laws of chemistry, and ideas in general. Among the wonderful things in life are those in the non-material realm: hope, friendship, patience, kindness, courage, honesty, integrity, comradeship, beauty, love, and the ideas presented in books, poetry, music, and art. Without such *things* as these, life would be vacant beyond comprehension. These "raw materials" which our minds use (mind-stuff) belong entirely in the mental realm. Books, which present ideas, consist largely of cellulose and printer's ink and thus have a material basis, but their essence is in the mind-nourishing ideas they contain. Songbirds and playful kittens, puppies, monkeys, and children have a material basis, but they charm us because they tickle and captivate our minds.

Nature's laws are certainly non-material; we grasp them only with our minds and they therefore fall into the category of mind-stuff. We can now learn these laws out of books, but although they are presumably eternal, it was originally human observation and the use of human minds that brought about their discovery. Archimedes discovered an important law while taking a bath. Newton discovered another while under an apple tree. These laws, which are *food for thought*, were presumably in operation for millennia before Archimedes and Newton were born. They were, from the beginning, by nature, *Gedankenstoffe*.

The mind-nourishing things in the world around us are supremely important from the standpoint of human existence—human happiness, human progress, and human betterment. They are as real as anything we know about, and it is unthinkable that we should exclude them from human knowledge.

To illustrate other laws of Nature which belong in the group of *Gedankenstoffe*, let us consider the phenomena of gravitation and motion. Gravitation is a physical force involving material things resulting from the fact that every particle in the universe attracts every other particle. There is, however, something else to gravitation besides material things and physical force. There are the laws, rules, and regulations which govern how gravitation works. These laws or rules are non-material; we cannot see, hear, touch, or taste them. They constitute a mind-food or mind-stuff which we must learn to cope with. On earth, we cannot escape the gravitational field in which we live, and our minds help us to accommodate to it. The laws of gravitation and motion affect all our movement and our bodily functions such as blood circulation. Without cooperating with these laws we could not walk or run, as we have already pointed out, because walking and running involve falling forward, under the influence of gravity, and successively catching ourselves with each succeeding step. This intangible mind-food which helps us cope with gravitation and the laws of motion keeps us from stepping off rooftops and from falling off cliffs or promontories when we climb mountains.

Mind-stuff is a marvelous thing because it appears to operate wherever matter exists. Every drop of water in the ocean and every grain of sand or pebble on the beach is endowed with a built-in responsiveness—a receptiveness or "sensitivity"—to the laws of gravitation and motion and obeys these laws automatically with mathematical accuracy. Nature must speak to them in some unknown "language" that they can understand because, as a matter of fact, not fiction, they do respond. Individual atoms and molecules are not as dead as they seem. They too respond when Nature instructs them as to how they are to behave.

There are many attractive forces in the universe besides gravitation (which is universal and acts even at great distances). Among these are very interesting close-range attractions (and repulsions) which may be negligible at distances of a millimeter or more but very strong at distances of a millimicron (one micron is a thousandth of a millimeter). These forces, unlike gravitation, are highly specific; their existence and strength depend on what kind of matter is involved. Since every atom and molecule has its own unique "likes and dislikes," there are many sets of "rules of conduct" which apply when one kind of molecule approaches another molecule of the same kind or a different kind. These "rules of conduct" or "mini-laws" are also

Gendankenstoffe—things we can comprehend with our minds. The rules themselves are non-material but crucially important and appear to exist, as we have said, wherever matter exists.

Water molecules, for example, are built to follow the mini-laws which Nature has prescribed for them. In effect, Nature tells water molecules how to behave under thousands of different contingencies. If a water molecule (H_2O) bumps into another of the same kind, it is instructed to join up with it and become $(H_2O)_2$. When an H_2O molecule encounters an $(H_2O)_2$ molecule, it is instructed to join together with it and to become an $(H_2O)_3$ molecule, This polymerization of H_2O is limited. Trimers and tetramers are common, but this is about as far as polymerization usually goes. When an H_2O molecule encounters a molecule of ammonia it is instructed to join up with it as it would with a molecule of water, and ammonium hydroxide results. When an H_2O molecule meets up with a carbon dioxide molecule, it joins up with it (weakly) to form carbonic acid. Nature instructs water molecules to adhere to hydrophilic (water-loving) substances and avoid hydrophobic (water-hating) substances.

The "instructions" that water receives from Nature are mere illustrations. Every kind of atom and molecule on earth has its instructions too, and these instructions are unique for each species. A sodium atom or a sodium ion acts as it does because it has appropriate, built-in "instructions" from Nature.

Close-range forces among atoms and molecules, parts of molecules, and even sub-atomic particles are universal as well as highly distinctive. If we express by N the number of *kinds* of centers of attraction (or repulsion) that exist, I calculate that the minimum number of sets of "rules of conduct," S, is given by the equation $S = N^2/2 + N/2$. If as few as 2,000 *kinds* of centers exist in the universe, there would be at least 2,001,000 *unique*, highly diverse sets of specific "rules of conduct" governing their approach to each other.

The existence of these distinctive forces (which are often very strong) is very much apparent in connection with the functioning of enzymes. Thousands of distinctive enzyme molecules (protein in nature) have in their structure "active sites" which selectively attract specific kinds of molecules and cause them to react chemically. We do not, for the most part, know the nature of these active sites, but their existence makes enzyme action possible. When we denature an enzyme (its structure unwinds), the active site disappears, but it reappears if we allow the enzyme to wind itself up again spontaneously, utilizing its own internal attractions. These enzymes and their specific active sites are essential cogs in the machinery of all life processes.

Scientists who think solely in terms of matter and energy cannot begin to fathom such problems as the origin of life on earth or the evolution of higher forms of life, including human beings. Probably the less these scientists say or write on such subjects, the better. With a broader view, which encompasses *Gedankenstoffe*, we shall see a little later that the origin of life and the evolution of higher forms are credible processes which fall in with Nature's way of doing things, even though mystery regarding life still exists.

Some mechanistic scientists may have highly exaggerated ideas about what can happen by mere chance. For example, it has been suggested that if an army of monkeys were strumming on typewriters in a random fashion, they might, given enough time, write all the books in the British Museum. This statement led me to calculate, partially for my own amusement, how long it would take one monkey, pecking away at random, to typewrite correctly a sentence requiring 38 pecks, such as, "Evolution takes place by mere chance." Since there are about 90 different pecking possibilities on a typewriter, the chance that the first peck would be the correct one would be one in 90; the chance that the first two pecks would be right would be one in 90^2; the chance that the first three pecks would be correct would be one in 90^3 (729,000). On this basis, the chance of the entire sentence being correct would be one in 90^{38}.

To simplify the calculations and speed up the writing as much as possible, we will assume that a monkey makes 38 pecks every ten seconds, pecking randomly and using the typewriter correctly, and would work 24 hours a day without a sleep break or a banana break, and that he had an "overseer" who would slip in a fresh slip of paper after each 38 pecks. To make 90^{38} trials would take at least 5,800,000,000,000,000,000,000,000,000,000,000,000,000,000, 000,000,000,000 billion years, wear out at least 2,900,000,000, 000,000,000,000,000,000,000,000,000,000,000,000,000,000,000 monkeys and a comparable number of overseers and typewriters. It would require using up paper weighing many times more than our entire solar system.

All of this effort would probably produce a correct copy of the sentence, but to search out from the many billions of tons of paper the slip with the correct sentence on it might require many, many billions of lifetimes of humans who could proofread and recognize it.

Bearing in mind our illustration of the monkeys who by aimless pecking on a typewriter could not possibly write a book, let us think about the possibility of atoms and molecules as dead pellets of matter aimlessly bouncing around in a random fashion producing the tremendous organization contained in a living cell with its metabolic machinery, proteins, enzymes, DNAs, mitochondria, and other organelles. It seems perfectly preposterous that all of this could have happened by chance during the few billion years since the earth took shape.

When, however, we consider the true nature of atoms and molecules and the highly complicated, built-in, specific instructions they receive from Nature, the picture changes most dramatically; it becomes an entirely different one. The moment *Gedankenstoffe* and intelligence enter the picture, the origin of life and the evolution of higher forms become possible. If the rules relating to the close-range forces did not exist, there could be no enzymes, no genetic codes, no reproduction, no life. The "rules of conduct" with respect to the close-range forces between molecules is the key without which life could never have originated or evolved. No *Gedankenstoffe*, no life!

Looked at from this point of view, the origin of life and the evolution of life are incredibly beautiful processes and presumably stem from an "infinite intellect." Albert Einstein is quoted as saying, "I want to know how God created the world. . . . I want to know His thoughts." So do we all. It seems that the biological world came into being because the atoms and molecules were specifically designed so as to have built-in instructions that made the origin of life and evolution happen. Could Erasmus have had something like this in mind when he said, "The dice of the gods are always loaded"?

Numerous *Gedankenstoffe* confront us in our lives and these are of great variety. Not all of them have the status of natural laws; some are mere *ideas* which we may be able to accept or reject. Some have become lodged in people's minds. These ideas are not uniformly beneficial. Hate, for example, can often poison our minds.

When certain ideas become widely accepted—as, for example, some "old wives tales" are—their acceptance exerts social pressure on still others to accept them. Such ideas I will call *"psychodes."* These psychodes are in the realm of *Gedankenstoffe*, and they may be highly influential social forces. All scientists and scholars need to recognize them as well as the whole gamut of *Gedankenstoffe*.

One of the most important long-standing psychodes is with respect to the status of women. In a number of cultures women are subordinate to men and are not always thought worthy of consideration. When my mother was a girl in Buffalo, New York, after the Civil War, she was valedictorian of her high school class, and I remember her showing me a large gold medal she received on this occasion. However, it never occurred to her father, an intelligent gentleman, to provide her with a college education; in those days it was not "the thing to do," due to the prevalence of the *idea* (psychode) "Women are subordinate to men." At that time, of course, women could not vote. This was a result of accepting the same idea. We find that this attitude persists today and profoundly influences the lives of men as well as women.

Another psychode: imagine, for a moment, a black child growing up in a society that believes blacks are inferior to whites. Regardless of whether there is any truth at all behind the idea, the child would have to live with this psychode continuously. Communication of the idea would most often be non-verbal, but it would affect him or her at all times. It would be difficult, if not impossible, for the black child to hold his or her head up and achieve his or her greatest potential while enveloped in this cloud. Here again is an intangible which greatly influences the lives of many people.

During the 19th century, when Britain was very much involved in the slave trade, a convenient, persistent psychode existed: "Slavery must be all right; everybody is doing it." Among the Quakers and Mennonites, however, there was a contrary over-riding psychode; these people evidently listened to their own consciences and concluded that "Slavery is wrong, and we will have no part of it." These two psychodes were in conflict for decades. Now the prevalent psychode is that which the Quakers and Mennonites entertained. No one

can question that these two psychodes have been tremendously
influential in history.

During the days of Hitler in Germany, a despicable psychode was
implanted in many minds: "Jews are an arrogant and power-hungry
people and inferior to Aryans." This psychode could not have developed if the youth of Germany had received a unified education. This
education would have convinced them that no ethnic group has a
uniform population. A homogeneous, uniform group of human
beings cannot exist as long as the laws of biology exist. No blanket
condemnation of Jews or any other group could withstand scrutiny
in the light of unified education.

The *Gedankenstoffe* that people receive during youth may easily
shape their entire lives.

Hope, as a non-material thing-of-the-mind, is one of the important
psychodes in our lives. We have succeeded in our country in estab-
lishing hope as one of the foundations of our society. People have
flocked to our country for generations because it has been a country
of hope and opportunity—a country where hopes for the future often
become realized—and the prevalence of this psychode of hope is a
strong attraction. We do not have to keep people from leaving our
country, nor do we prohibit it. Our main trouble has been keeping
too many from entering. This is because the psychode of hope and
freedom prevails and seems to be in the very air we breathe. Another
psychode which makes our country attractive is the idea that we
should live here in mutual respect with a sense of belonging. As long
as these important psychodes exist in our minds, our country will be
a haven for the oppressed.

Love, of course, is the greatest psychode of all. Parents do love
their children, spouses do love each other, and even secular-minded
people often have a deep-seated love for mankind.

But there are two more psychodes which I wish to discuss specifically because of their great importance. One of these is the psychode
of honesty and integrity. It makes a vast difference in our society and
in our country when people have this psychode. In my experience as a
scientist, it would be *unthinkable* by custom and strong tradition for
any reputable scientist to misread his measuring instruments deliberately in order to make the results of his experiment more acceptable
and impressive. This psychode is, in the field of Science, extremely

strong and universal, and one's "religious" beliefs or lack of them have no connection with it. Without this psychode, science would crumble and fail utterly. This psychode also carries over to other activities. A professional golfer, for example, binds himself to the rules of the game and scrupulously follows them even though in specific instances they may be greatly to his disadvantage. Even when many thousands of dollars may be at stake, professional golfers have called penalties on themselves as a matter of course although no one else could possibly have seen the reason for the penalty. This psychode, or sense of decency, is absolutely invaluable.

The psychode of honesty and integrity is not only essential in science and in the game of golf, but also in citizenship, in business, in politics, and in all of life. If the members of a society lack this psychode, that society is like a house built on a foundation of shifting sands. When numerous highly selected military cadets cheat on examinations, this is a serious danger-signal. When reputable colleges and universities doctor their records to promote athletic eligibility, this is also a bad sign. When cheating in a university is readily excusable and later does not stand in the way of one's becoming an acceptable candidate for the Presidency, and when a President of the United States has to admit that he lied, we should become *seriously* concerned about the weakness of the psychode of honesty and integrity. We should be vitally concerned with strengthening and building up this psychode in all individuals, young and old, as much as possible. Even in our present imperfect world, some sense of honesty and integrity is absolutely essential for doing business of any kind.

The other psychode that I wish to mention specifically I will call the "moral optimism" psychode. When we have this psychode we are deeply convinced that in the long run truth will outlast falsehood, that beauty will take precedence over ugliness and that right is better than wrong. This is a psychode which may be regarded as highly desirable for everyone, especially if we do not attempt to define the terms truth, beauty, and right too rigidly.

Some other psychodes worth thinking about are the following: 1) Hard work is something to be avoided. 2) "All one needs is a balanced diet." 3) "Right" is what one *thinks* is right. 4) Sex is a marvelous fun-thing. 5) Religion is a crutch for stupid people. 6) A charismatic person who speaks as though he *knows*, cannot be wrong. 7) Everything in print must be true. 8) Classical music is unimaginative and is a thing of the past. 9) Poetry is for sissies. 10) Of all the toothpastes (or beers, face creams, electric razors, etc.) on the market, there must be one that is really the best.

All these psychodes and more should be considered in unified education. There is such a thing as social contagion, and this may be constructive. Psychodes are related to the phenomena of "crowd psychology," "mob psychology," and "gang psychology"—phenomena which we must investigate and understand while pursuing a unified education.

Chapter XI

Enlightenment for the Professions

Members of the professions and the many millions of people who depend upon them will suffer the most if the new unified education is not forthcoming. By "professions" I mean those occupations requiring special training which deal directly with people and serve them in many life situations.

If a member of the professions—a minister, priest, rabbi, attorney, judge, physician, educator—thinks primarily about *the* layman, *the* client, *the* patient, or *the* student, he or she cannot do a decent job. Such a professional would be like a shoe merchant who can furnish only one size of shoe, an optician who fits everyone with the same prescription, or the restaurateur who is prepared to serve only one menu.

If one does not know individuality he cannot possibly know people and their needs. Every successful member of a profession knows, by intuition or observation, *something* about individuality. Usually, however, it is only a minute fraction of what he or she should know. The new unified education brings to the fore such *facts* (not speculations) about individuality as those presented at the end of Chapter IV. In order to serve people satisfactorily, professionals have to know people as they really are. They, like shoe merchants, opticians, and restaurateurs, have to serve individuals. If they know very little about these individuals and their particular needs, they cannot serve them. At best, they can only fumble around in their attempts to help others. Common sense tells us that the new unified education which considers adequately the facts of individuality should be furnished to every prospective member of the professions as a part of his or her basic training and that present members of the professions should be alerted to these same facts. Every member of every profession needs to know the undeniable fact that ignorance about individuality spells ignorance about people.

Besides those who deal with shoes, eyeglasses, and prepared meals, others, including all professionals, must know that individual needs may be highly distinctive and different. If they do not know this, the ministers, priests, and rabbis will be totally ineffective as counselors; attorneys will give inappropriate legal advice; judges will make misjudgements; physicians will cause wholesale iatrogenic (physician-induced) disease; educators will fail to give students the kinds of education they need. One student may learn in six minutes what another student will fail to learn in six years. This is a part of individuality.

The study of individuality will bring a new dimension to practitioners of every profession—that of understanding themselves and the people whom they seek to serve. Prospective professionals must first study their own minds and temperaments to help determine whether they are suitable candidates for a particular profession, and then they must study the individuality of those whom they wish to serve.

It has been a scandalous short-sightedness, lasting for centuries, that has kept us so long in ignorance of individuality. The training of medical professionals in this regard, for example, has been sorely neglected. As mentioned in Chapter IV, in 1956 I published a book entitled *Biochemical Individuality* which was widely distributed and translated. This book stressed innate differences in the field of biochemistry but also called attention to individual differences with respect to anatomy, genetics, sensory physiology, pharmacology, endocrinology, nutrition, and psychology. Yet I venture that not more than one physician in ten has ever faced squarely the information that this book contains about how, in many areas, differences are by no means trivial. These differences do not involve only a few percentage points—often the variations, even in organ weights, are more than ten-fold in magnitude.

In unifying knowledge it is most important to note that while bits-and-pieces of individuality are seen in many specialities, it is only through unification that medical professionals and others can appreciate individuality as a crucial fact of life. Since fragmented science has no use for the word *individuality*, unified science is required to call attention to its existence and to make it comprehensible. The recognition of individuality is in line with the historical "quotation" from the physician Parry of Bath: "It is more important to know what kind of a person has a disease than it is to know what kind of a disease a person has."

It is also worth noting at this point that *no physician ever had a patient who was not a highly distinctive individual.* And each individual needs to be treated as a whole, not as a collection of fragments. The grassroots "holistic health" movement is characterized by its attention to this point.

This individuality has a firm basis in anatomy because, as Barry Anson has shown in his *Atlas of Human Anatomy* (1951), human bodies differ from each other strikingly in hundreds of different ways. It is not an accident that "one person's meat may be another's poison." Biological variability greatly complicates medical science, but medical scientists must realistically face the facts of unified knowledge with respect to individuality. Many medical problems will continue to be unsolvable as long as we sweep individuality under the rug.

In the new unified education there is another area related to medical training which has been sorely neglected in our traditional education. One of the most elementary facts of life, as we have pointed out, is that our environment is supremely important, mainly because there are crucial chemical exchanges between our environment and ourselves. Prospective medical scientists should be fully acquainted with these facts early in life and long before they enter the portals of a medical school. These exchanges ordinarily involve the air we breathe, the water we drink, and the food we eat. The principle involved is simple. Unless we get the right chemicals from our environment we cannot continue to live or develop; if we get the wrong chemicals from our air, water, and food we may even die as a result.

In the light of these statements, it is a curious fact that medical scientists are, generally speaking, not well versed with respect to the chemicals we need to get in our food and water. Nor are they as expert as they should be with respect to the wrong chemicals that can impair our faculties and kill us.

A major part of the concern of my own life work as a scientist has been in finding chemicals (nutrients) that we need to get from our environment, and in persuading the medical scientists and practitioners that these substances require their careful consideration in connection with the promotion of health and the avoidance of disease. Because nutritional considerations are interdisciplinary in nature, fragmented science never does justice to nutrition. As a result, pre-medical education is always inadequate, and pre-medical students are crippled (perhaps even for life) by a lack of appreciation of the Grand Scheme of Nature and the indispensability of all the nutrients in the promotion of life and health.

Still another area in which medical training demands more unified knowledge is with respect to the psychodes. Few medical practioners would want to deny that what people think very often greatly influences their health. It is my impression, however, that most physicians are not optimistic nor satisfied with respect to their ability to help their patients by guiding their thinking. Psychodes influence people's lives tremendously and in many ways, but we need more and better experts who are well rounded in the field of practical and remedial psychology. A more intensive development of unified education and its incorporation into medical science will help to fill this need.

We have used the medical profession as an example, and it is evident that unified education can do wonders for it and all the people who patronize it. The same principles hold for other professions and the people they serve. Individual needs of every kind can be met with *far greater satisfaction* if unified education, including adequate knowledge about individuality, enters into all pre-professional and professional training.

Chapter XII

Where Will Unified Education Lead Us?

If we follow through in our thinking with unified education as a basis, what will be the outcome? Will we become cynical, materialistic, and lose our idealism, our humanity, our altruism, our love of home and country, and our love of family and friends? Quite the opposite, because every door will be wide open to constructive thinking and we will have a new sense of balance—which, with our customary education, we are sorely lacking.

I can think of no better way to seek the unbiased truth than to proceed, step by step, to understand as best we can everything in the world that affects our lives. Unified education does exactly this; it is pragmatic. It will help us apply this knowledge in a practical manner to our lives and will help us to select the courses of action which best suit our individual needs and tastes.

With unified education we will know how to care better for our bodies and our minds. As a result, we will be able to think straighter and use our minds to the utmost—perhaps to study *Gedankenstoffe* in ways which we have previously never used.

Will unified education lead us toward a new interest in religion and a belief in God? Quite possibly. Sir Fred Hoyle, a leading astronomer of Cambridge University, has thrown light on the present situation by saying that the existence of an enormous intelligence abroad in the universe is palatable to most ordinary folk but exceedingly unpalatable to scientists. Physical scientists do not characteristically say (out loud), "There is no God," but they often teach the idea effectively by ignoring even the possiblity that God exists. From the standpoint of unified education this attitude is completely unscientific, fundamentally misleading, and, in a sense, dishonest.

There are many indications that the idea of "an enormous intelligence abroad in the universe" is being taken seriously at the present time by more than a few physical scientists and philosophers. In his speech at California Institute of Technology in July 1981, Sir Fred Hoyle himself endorsed the idea.

In Chapter V we quoted Max Planck, Werner Heisenberg, and Albert Einstein as presupposing the existence of an "infinite intellect."

In the article, "Rediscovering the Mind" also mentioned in Chapter V, Harold J. Morowitz states, "How remarkable it is that the scientific study of the world led to the content of consciousness as an ultimate reality." In other words, the mind is a prime factor in life, in which case a Supreme Intellect is not unreasonable.

In 1976 Benjamin Pinkel, an engineer, published a book, *The Existential Adventure*, (DeVorss & Co.) in which he set forth the idea that the universe not only contains matter and energy, but also a phenomenological field, called "phenofield" for short. While he did not spell out exactly what he would include in the phenofield, I am sure he intended to include mathematical principles, natural laws, and the like. A Supreme Intellect fits in perfectly with his ideas about the "phenofield."

James Horigan has published a book, *Chance or Design* (Philosophical Library, Inc., 1979), in which he strongly defends the existence of a designing intellect behind the universe.

Dr. John Smith, Clark Professor of Philosophy at Yale, has recently published an article, "Science and Conscience" (*American Scientist*, September-October 1980). He emphasizes the thought that, as we increase our knowledge, our consciences are sharpened. Since conscience is often interpreted as the "voice of God," his discussion is in line with the idea of a Supreme Intellect and moral force.

This interest in religion and the existence of God has even made the headlines in prominent news magazines. In *Time* magazine is an article entitled, "Modernizing the Case for God" (April 7, 1980, p. 65). In the March 9, 1981 issue (p. 72) of *Newsweek*, a prominent article appears entitled, "A 'Nobel' for the Spiritual."

The awarding of the Nobel prize in Chemistry to Ilya Prigogine, as I mentioned in Chapter V, for work which throws light on biology and sociology is further evidence of an increasing openness of mind regarding fundamental philosophical problems.

It will be evident to every person with a unified education that God does not exist with a material body; no one has seen God at any time. A person with a unified education, however, will reflect that no one has ever seen a mathematical principle or a law of motion or other natural laws at any time. Neither has anyone at any time seen hope, honesty, or love. Yet, the same person with a unified education will know that all these things exist in reality and are highly pertinent to life.

It is obvious that anyone who is seeking to find a "Supreme Intelligence" will not find this with a telescope or any similar instrument. Possibly entirely new tools will be developed in the future which will enable us to probe into the unseen and to study the all-important *Gedankenstoffe*.

Personally, I cannot help but wonder whether, when we think straight in the field of mathematics and science and have valuable intuition, when our consciences tell us emphatically what is right, when we have generous impulses, when beautiful poetry emanates from the personality of an Emily Dickinson, when newly created music flows from the soul of George Gershwin, are not these the echoes from a Master Mind and a Master Soul?

These wonderings are, in the light of my recognition of the nature and tremendous importance of what I have called psychodes, perfectly reasonable and perfectly scientific.

I am extremely reticent about telling others what they should or should not believe. My own personal experience, about which I should be perfectly frank and open, will help throw light upon what I have to say about religion. I have been influenced by my upbringing, but I have also had a distinctive mind of my own and have accepted what I have thought to be true and rejected what I thought to be false.

I was born in India of Baptist missionaries. Both my father and mother were very much interested in what they were doing, and I absorbed a religious training from them and inherited biologically from them some of the mental characteristics that made them become missionaries.

When I was a boy of eight years, living in the town of Eureka, Kansas, I recognized my responsibilities in a new light and on my own, without parental persuasion, enthusiastically joined the Christian fold. While as a prospective Baptist I was not asked to accept any creed, I was at the time mysteriously touched by a love that has never left me through a long life of many vicissitudes and imperfections and a few severe traumas.

My questioning attitude over a lifetime is illustrated by a mild and rather one-sided dispute I had with my parents rather early in life. I took the position that since God is a spirit (this my parents could not deny), Jesus, if he were God, must have been God in spirit. His body was not God. Accordingly, I argued that what happened to Jesus' *body* after he was crucified was not of great import. What was important was whether his spirit survived.

Long before I graduated from college I entertained many heresies, but they did not interfere with my faith in a God of love. I thank God fervently, but I hope not piously, for the peace of mind I have usually enjoyed through many years. I covet for other members of the human family the beneficient inner peace which I fortunately possess.

As we have indicated in several chapters of this book, unified education has great potentialities for bringing people together in many ways. There is even a strong probability that unified education will lead us to a new and different goal which we can attain in no other way—a non-sectarian, ecumenical religion. If so, it will not be a religion shot through with superstititions and, because it will fully recognize human individuality, it will not be the kind of religion which causes us to persecute and kill those who do not agree with us. Presumably, every existing religion has some valuable features and there seems to be no good reason why these features cannot be recognized and coalesced, leaving room, however (as, for example, in the Roman Catholic Church), for differing views with respect to points of emphasis. This new ecumenical religion would be acceptable to a host of Jews, Christians, Mohammedans, and others, including giants of the past of the stature of Abraham Lincoln, Thomas Jefferson, Leo Tolstoy, and François Voltaire. As a youngster I was brought up to think of Voltaire as an atheist—one of the bad guys—but I added his name to the above list because he said, "If God did not exist, it would be necessary to invent Him." On his death bed, when the abbé refused him absolution, he drew up a statement which he gave to his secretary, Wagner: "I die adoring God, loving my friends, not hating my enemies, and detesting superstition [signed] Voltaire. February 28, 1778."

I am sure that many scientists, philosophers, and scholars of the present day regard spirituality as an empty dream. How can they be convinced of this empty dream unless they see the *whole* picture? How can they see the whole picture unless they have a unified education? A unified education can hopefully bring us much new knowledge. For example, at present we do not have any knowledge about where intuitions and ideas come from. Perhaps if we could see the whole picture clearly, we would know that *Gedankenstoffe* such as intuitions and ideas come from the "infinite intellect" in the universe and we could learn to tap more effectively this vast resource.

Who knows?

Chapter XIII

Prevention of War

Prevention of war is a tough problem, but unified education is made to order to help solve it.

Many people have often said that making war on each other is one of the most senseless and immoral things we human beings do. This is particularly pertinent to our present situation because we have a real threat of an atomic holocaust which may obliterate a substantial part of the human race. Since I have written a book on the prevention of alcoholism (as I mentioned on p. 47), prevention is very much on my mind, and to prevent war is extremely urgent. In order to prevent something we have to know what its roots are and how to cope with them. We can take for granted that the better the understanding

119

people have of each other the less cause there will be for war. People are always individuals in their thinking and attitudes and, without an appreciation of the fact that individuality is inborn and inescapable, they have great difficulty in getting along with each other. Once they appreciate the facts of biological individuality, however, they are in a position to deal with each other and appreciate each other in a sense that would be impossible without this knowledge.

We human beings are all together in this world. Some are more fortunate than others, and some appear to be saints, though most of us are not. Neither are we complete villains. We all stumble through life in spite of common imperfections and uncertainties. When we fully realize this, it gives us a strong fellow-feeling for each other. We appreciate each other more and this opens the door for friendliness.

Groups of people in different cultures have distinctive tastes and attitudes and they tend to go to war with each other because of intolerance, hatred, and conflict of interest. These attitudes are fostered by ignorance about human individuality. Whatever we can do to make people more tolerant and understanding with respect to their neighbors will help us move in the direction of "no more war." The emphasis in this book on "things we can agree upon," and the building of common knowledge makes for more friendly relations. Most of this book has to do at least indirectly with the prevention of war.

Does psychology have anything to do with war? Some would say that psychology has everything to do with war; war always starts in people's minds. Does "crowd psychology" have anything to do with war? Don't we need to know more about it? Is economics a cause of war? Some might say that most wars have an economic base. To what extent does the industrial production of guns, ammunition, etc., promote war? Certainly, under present circumstances, there is a demand for guns, ammunition, tanks, airplanes, and submarines on the part of countries which are not in a good position to produce them. Do education and the training of youth have anything to do with war? If in doubt, look at Hitler's regime. Does religion have anything to do with war? Many wars have had religious origins. However, one Christian sect, the Quakers, consult their consciences and protest the existence of war and will not support or have anything to do with it. Do food supply and food quality have anything to do with war? In some cases, certainly. The acquisition of food is a prime urge and the quality of one's food has a great deal to do with emotions and health. Is overcrowding likely to precipitate war? Many regard this as one of the prominent factors in promoting war. Communist China has made an important step toward the prevention of war by discouraging couples from having more than one child. India, on the other hand, has never had the gumption to adopt this practice. Effective prevention of war may involve finding acceptable ways whereby people will not repeatedly bring children into the world unless they are prepared to give them a good start in life (as I mentioned on p. 50) and provide for them adequately in every way. Do individuality and the psychology of leadership have anything to do with war? Do not the cases of Napoleon and Hitler prove that this is so? (One of the incidental objections to war is that it tends to crush individuality. Soldiers ideally should be the same size, wear the same type of uniform, shoot the same way, and march in perfect unison.) Can we relate the enjoyment of boxing and of violence in TV shows to war? I think so. Can it be that the psychologies of men and women are sufficiently different so that it is true that "if women had their way there would be no more war"? If female psychology is that different, one possible expedient in the prevention of war would be to give women more power and the ability to veto every act or declaration of war. Would it be possible to enlist the women of the world in a movement to prevent war? The question of whether sociology and politics have anything to do with war almost answers itself.

In the solving of problems *that involve material things*—like energy, protecting our environment, and the *how* of making war— our culture has many potentialities. We have thousands of specialists trained in these matters who are in a position to give enormous help.

In solving the problem of preventing war, however, *where human factors are dominant*, our culture has not provided us with experts trained to solve such complex problems. We need broad-gauged experts who know about the material *and* the human factors— psychology, economics, industry, munitions, education, religions, food supply, overcrowding, individuality, leadership, sociology, politics, etc.—and who can see all these factors in perspective.

Here is where unified education enters. The only way we can have experts of the kind we need to make a thorough investigation of the cause of war and the ways to prevent it is to coordinate our learning and blend together the various disciplines into a unified education. Fragmentary, bit-by-bit knowledge cannot be a solid basis for studying the causes of war and the prevention of the disasters which come with war. If we choose not to develop unified education we are probably choosing a continuance of wars which may lead to our annihilation. Somehow our culture must foster the production of great men and women, not specialized "educated idiots." This is a challenge to our culture and to all other cultures, and we can do it only if we develop and foster unified education.

Human nature being what it is, no one is in a position to make a guarantee that if we do certain things this will eliminate war. It is not that simple. If, however, we develop tremendous new insights into human nature by means of unified education, and if we *try* expertly to knit the peoples of the earth together through a unified body of knowledge, we will have a much better chance of preventing war.

Chapter XIV

What Change Can We Expect?

In the previous thirteen chapters of this book we have stressed the advantages of unified education and the weaknesses inherent in education when it is incomplete, fragmented, and disjointed. Now I propose to discuss briefly how unification can be brought about, starting with education as it exists today.

If education is to move in the direction of more unification, the first step seems perfectly clear. Scholars and educators in substantial numbers must be thoroughly convinced that a coherent education is vastly better than an incoherent one and that the world will be better off in a thousand ways if this coherence can be attained. As soon as this crucial conviction is widespread, education will begin to move toward the desired goal of unification and coherence. This conviction is so vital that without it education must remain fragmented indefinitely.

There is no practicality whatever in the idea that a governing board, chancellor, president, or dean can say to a faculty, "From now on we are going to promote unified education." Academic freedom is absolutely essential and indeed very real. Every educator is, or should be, trained to do his or her own thinking and use his or her own best judgement. Good educators always learn from others, but it is obligatory that they have judgements of their own.

My own personal experience (at the university level) has demonstrated to me how vital academic freedom is. When I first began teaching organic chemistry sixty-five years ago at the University of Oregon (Eugene), I found out immediately that I could not teach the subject as I had been taught it at the University of Redlands, the University of California at Berkeley, or at the University of Chicago—where I had received my doctorate degree one year earlier. I had to teach it *my own way*. For one thing, I realized organic chemistry had been taught as though it were a story by itself, separate from all other chemistry. One of my earliest publications, in 1923, combatted this idea. After seven years at the University of Oregon, I published a textbook on organic chemistry which embodied *my way* of teaching the subject. It had enough appeal so that it was used in over 300 colleges and universities, including Yale, Princeton, and Dartmouth, during its first year. (This book was in direct competition with one on the same subject written by James B. Conant, the future President of Harvard University.) The widespread use of my book (five editions) was the primary factor in my being elected, exactly thirty years after its publication, as President of the American Chemical Society. This book and its subsequent wide influence could not have come into existence if a healthy academic freedom had not prevailed in my mind and in the University of Oregon. On principle, no competent educator should be asked to promote unified education (or anything else) against his better judgment.

Those scholars and educators who are not particularly impressed by the idea of unified education will obviously do nothing to promote it. But those who *are* impressed by the idea will, just as obviously, seek to further it. I think I know my colleagues in education well enough to be assured that those who realize the tremendous advantages of unified education will not deliberately deliver fragmented education to their students.

My sustained efforts (Chapters I to XIII) to convince scholars and educators of the advantages of a complete and coherent education are fully justified because, if all these key people remain unconvinced, the promotion of unified education will certainly fail.

In order to move in the direction of unified education, it will not be necessary to abolish departments or take other drastic steps in reorganization. In most instances, departments can be left virtually as they are. The practice of having individuals hold professorships in more than one department might well become more prevalent.

One of the things that interested scholars and teachers can do is to emphasize in their classrooms, conversations, scholarly publications, and books background material which will help place their particular discipline in perspective with regard to other disciplines. Teachers in elementary schools and high schools should ideally include background material and place in perspective every new subject they introduce.

Another move (at the university level) would be to foster enlightening and provocative inter-departmental seminars at both the undergraduate and graduate levels. Still another would be to invite, as university lecturers, men and women with breadth of learning. One device which might be used to induce students to think more intensely and digest what they are learning would involve asking them periodically to hand in for consideration general *questions* to which they would like answers. A course which does not stimulate original questions in students' minds is not much of a course.

One of the objectives of forward-looking educators might be a much intensified interest in history (this could start even at the elementary and high school levels)—the history of mathematics, the history of physics, the history of chemistry, the history of biology, the histories of political science, economics, languages, music, etc. History, according to my conception, must be brought to life and be made more meaningful, instead of merely being a series of dates and events to be memorized, and should naturally include penetrating contacts with human beings who have made major contributions. No one who has a knowledge of the histories of a dozen different disciplines could be regarded as an uneducated person.

At the University of Texas, Professor John A. Wheeler, recently from Princeton, has introduced a course, "Great Men, Great Moments, and Great Ideas in Physics," which must have the effect of bringing physics into better perspective. Courses somewhat parallel to this one might well be instituted in many departments in any university when there are suitable individuals to teach them.

The idea of unified education is contagious and if it once catches on, it will probably spread gradually, over a period of years, to the whole teaching profession at all levels.

Even at the present time, I cannot imagine a top economist taking the position that his expertise is based on his deep concentration on economics to the exclusion of "non-essentials"—psychology, group psychology, political science, law, and ethics. Neither can I imagine an outstanding psychologist having no regard for biology, ethics, economics, and political science. Unity in education is already "in the air," and I predict that eventually "interdisciplinary" will cease to be a dirty word in educational organization.

Interdisciplinary research will surely become more respectable, especially when it is recognized that many human problems cannot be studied in depth and solved without it.

Let us consider at this time three specific outstanding human problems: 1) getting along together, 2) mental diseases and aberrations, 3) alcoholism and drug abuse. Now let us consider three questions with respect to each of these three problems. First, are genetics and heredity involved in the problem? Second, is psychology involved in the problem? Third, is biochemistry involved in the problem? The answer to all these questions in every case is "Yes, yes, yes." Since the answers are all affirmative, it should be perfectly clear that interdisciplinary research, at least including genetics and heredity, psychology and biochemistry, is absolutely essential to their thorough study and solution. There is no escape from this conclusion.

Under conditions which prevail at the present time, interdisciplinary research is well-nigh impossible. For an interdisciplinary project to receive financial support, it would have to be reviewed routinely by several panels of *specialists* representing several different disciplines. It probably would not be understood and approved by any one of the panels, let alone all of them.

One of the roots of unified education goes back to the early 1900s, when Dr. Maria Montessori, herself an interdisciplinarian—a physician and "pedagogical anthropologist"—founded the Montessori system of education. This takes into account a complete inventory of a child's makeup and seeks to educate children in every way. In Switzerland, public Montessori schools were established by law in 1911 and the principles on which they rest may be regarded as basic not only to elementary education but also to education at more advanced levels. One of the underlying principles of the Montessori system is that of individuality, which, as we have indicated (page 31), is one of the cornerstones of unified education. Every educated person should know not only about his or her *total* environment, but also about himself or herself as an individual person.

When education becomes more unified and more realistic, we will introduce into our school system courses specifically on the subjects of individuality. At the university level, if thoroughness is one objective, individuality inevitably belongs in the department of anthropology. A "science of man" which leaves out individuality is a misnomer and a subterfuge. Individuality belongs also in psychology (differential psychology) and is vital to it. Individuality also belongs in anatomy, physiology, and biochemistry. Individuality is absolutely inescapable in medicine. Eventually, perhaps not before the 21st century, individuality will be regarded as a legitimate field of study in the education process. At the present time it is looked upon, if at all, as a mere passing footnote.

The idea that the earth is a huge, roundish ball was at one time uncertain, but now is generally accepted as a fact. Why? Because it makes complete sense when thought of from every possible angle. The idea that a coherent education is vastly superior to an incoherent one should be in about the same range of certainty. It will eventually be generally accepted because it makes complete sense when looked at from every possible angle. It is built on solid thought processes and has within its own makeup the capability of correcting any temporary misconceptions. Unified education may take years and possibly decades for its importance to be fully digested, but its eventual acceptance—if man is to survive and progress—is almost as certain as the sunrise.

Some people have pessimistic blood in their veins and áre inclined to throw up their hands in dismay saying, "We have so many evil urges and this world is in such a complicated mess that there is no hope for straightening it out." My response is, "Let's try something new and different; there is still hope for the future if we really *try*."

Our expectations from this book can be summarized in one word—enlightenment. *How much* enlightenment there will be will depend upon the readers and the non-readers of this book. If educators, prominent opinion-makers, foundations, and people in highly responsible positions can make sense out of what I have been saying, and will speak, write, and act accordingly, there is no tellng how great this enlightenment will be.

I take comfort in the thought that education and statecraft are not likely to remain perfectly static and that there is likely to be movement and change. My native optimism leads me to expect, or at least to hope, that, as time goes on, education will become less fragmented, less specialized, and less picayunish rather than more so. I also hope that nations will in the future think *more* about good public relations rather than less. Granted, unifying changes may come more slowly than we would wish, yet I think they will come and we will actually move into a new age of enlightenment and amity.

I believe that the continuous knitting process we referred to in Chapter VII will go on and on. It seems psychologically sound to think that if neighboring nations find themselves in agreement on ten propositions, they will be more inclined rather than less inclined to reach an agreement on proposition number eleven, whatever it is.

My strategy has three outstanding advantages which bolster my optimism. First, it involves no coercion—it does not expect people to be different from what they are, and different cultures can give voice to their own virtues and perpetuate their attractive features. The second advantage of my strategy is that, while it appears pragmatically feasible and educationally sound, no one has ever attempted anything of this kind before; therefore, the word "failure" is not a part of its vocabulary. Thirdly, this plan is not a palliative or a superficial remedy; it strikes at the very roots of dissension, strife, and hatred. Groups of people hate and distrust each other largely because they have different educational backgrounds rather than because one group is virtuous and the other full of faults. If we do our best to give people a common core of non-controversial knowledge, we automatically get over a hurdle which prevents mutual trust and amity.

One very strong advantage of the strategy I present is that we need not judge its success on an all-or-nothing basis. If this plan operates in the direction of true enlightenment even to a small degree, it will be a success. If only a few people grasp the insights into ourselves and our environment provided by unified education and are thereby able to live more satisfactory lives, this book, for them and for me, will be a success.

There will certainly be resistance when one tries to implement the contents of this book. Many educators are used to the old ways and may have vested interests in them and want no fundamental changes in our educational system. This resistance must be challenged and overcome by peaceful persuasion. Resistance to change is a part of human nature.

It is possible that some individual or foundation with clout will find this new strategy compellingly sound and will see that it is brought to the attention of influential people in many cultures. Very often valuable new ideas do not receive immediate, spontaneous acceptance. Persistent "pushers" may be indispensable.

There are many voices besides mine in support of moving in the direction of unified education. I call attention here to (1) the Rockefeller Commission on the Humanities Report (see Appendix I); (2) Harold J. Morowitz's article (which I mentioned on page 38) entitled "Rediscovering the Mind" (*Psychology Today*, August 1980); (3) John E. Smith's article "Science and Conscience" (*American Scientist*, September-October 1980); (4) Prof. Fritz Machlup's eight volume compendium on Knowledge which I mentioned on page 39; (5) and editorial in *Science* entitled, "Affinities between Scientists and Humanists" (Apendix II); and (6) an editorial in *Science* entitled, "Usefulness of the Social Sciences" (Appendix III).

From these citations it is obvious that many prominent people, when presented with the idea of unified education, will be favorably disposed. There is strong reason for believing that the concept of unified education is "an idea whose time has come." There is absolutely no substitute for unified education, and it is so sound and so basic that there is little room for contrary argument. Some may be pessimistic about our ability to develop unified education but I think no one will think of it in any way except as highly desirable. The task of developing it will seem far less formidable when we actually give it a try.

I agree with the maxim of the Christophers: "It is better to light a candle than to curse the darkness." I have lighted my candle. Like other lighters of candles, I have a vast hope of success. This book is for the present and for the 21st century and beyond.

Postscript: a Challenge

Dear Readers:

One of my favorite notable correspondents, who has read this book in manuscript, has referred to it as a "clarion call." What do *you* do as a result of a clarion call? How do you respond? Well, whatever you do, I challenge you to do just that—and promptly.

We educators, and all educated people, are the real caretakers and guardians of humanity. No one else can do the job. We have the capability, for example, of nourishing pregnant women so that their offspring will have maximum potential, and of feeding our children and ourselves for maximum benefit. At present we do not *deliver* on either of these two capabilities. If we do not know immediately how

131

to do these things, we can, by careful study and research, find out how. We also have the capability of learning how to feed children and adults intellectually and spritually. We do not capitalize on this opportunity either.

As we move into a new age of enlightenment, all of us need to think seriously about unified education and translate our thought into action. Are we giving our youth and adults what they really need? Are we doing a 100% job? Or is it more like 80%? 60%? 40%? Or even less?

Our responsibilities in this matter do not extend beyond our capabilities—we all have capabilities beyond what we realize. At the age of eighty seven, when I started this book, I knew I wanted to write something along this line, but I had *no idea whatever*, in view of the fact that I had been legally blind for nine years, that I would be as successful as I have been in developing such an outstandingly important theme. You too can probably do more than you think you can!

The future of humanity is at stake. Please respond in any way that you can *now*, before it is too late.

Appendix I

The Rockefeller Foundation Commission on the Humanities

Under the leadership of the late John H. Knowles, M.D., the Rockefeller Foundation, "sharing with many people a profound disquiet about the state of the humanities in our culture," decided to appoint a Commission to assess the humanities' place and prospects. Richard W. Lyman, then President of Stanford University and now president of the Rockefeller Foundation, headed this distinguished Commission of thirty-one members. The University of California Press, Berkeley, published this Commission's Report under the title of *The Humanities in American Life* (1980, 191 pp.)

In summary, this Report indicates that the humanities suffer from inadequate attention and that we need to strengthen, support, and develop them at every turn—in elementary schools, high schools, colleges, and graduate education—not only through the agency of the schools themselves but also through museums, libraries, newspapers, television, and radio. The Commission was strongly pro-humanities, but I am sure it was not anti-science.

With this idea of being strongly pro-humanistic but not anti-science I am in total agreement. Everything in the humanities and in the social sciences can come under the purview of comprehensive World-Knowledge. This coordination and unification can be tremendously advantageous for education and it will solve the "humanities problem."

Also, I call attention to the extreme desirability for all scientists and humanists to consider the advantages of a sophisticated approach to the values of religion. It will be evident to the readers of this book that there is much in comprehensive World-Knowledge which points toward God.

Appendix II

Affinities between Scientists and Humanists

A Commission on the Humanities, sponsored by the Rockefeller Foundation, recently issued a report on the state and role of the humanities in American life. Scientists should take heed and take heart.

For possibly the first time, a diverse group of representatives of the humanities—from schools, colleges, and universities; from libraries, the media, and public life; from foundations, museums, and business—has summoned the humanities and modern liberal education to acknowledge, rather than flee, the realities and consequences

*This editorial appeared in *Science*, January 2, 1981, and is reprinted with permission.

135

of science and technology. "If the aim is to make invention creative and humane," the Commission insists, "knowledge of the humanities must be coupled with an understanding of the characteristics of scientific inquiry and technological change. Liberal education must define scientific literacy as no less important a characteristic of the educated person than reading and writing."

Yet, asserts the Commission, if humanists bear responsibilities, long disregarded, toward the sciences, so too scientists must accept reciprocal obligations toward the humanities. "When scientists and technicians are deeply concerned about questions raised by their unprecedented success in transforming the human environment, when questions of value, responsibility, and freedom can no longer be seen as falling outside the province of scientific activity, dialogue with humanists becomes increasingly important...To be a good scientist, one must be more than a scientific specialist."

Lest such truths become mere truisms, however, scientists and humanists must go beyond the Commission's injunction and accept the deep intellectual affinity between their fields. The sciences, like the humanities, are not merely subjects of study but also ways of pursuing knowledge in its many manifestations. Both—contrary to the self-congratulatory views of some people from both groups—represent the great achievements of the human mind and spirit. Both, in their distinctive manner, have created and revealed the beauties and awesome realities of nature and human civilization. It serves no purpose, nor is it accurate, to think otherwise.

Nor is it wise for scientists to depreciate the ingredients of judgement, intuition, and ambiguity in the work of the humanities or for the humanists to conceive of science and technology as the products of mere positivism. As we now know, the intellectual grandeur and predicaments shared by the sciences and humanities are as numerous and profound as the qualities and problems that may distinguish them. Scholars in both worlds confront the fragmentation and uncertainty of all knowledge and are faced with weak public understanding and declining support. And both scientists and humanists know the peril of claiming too much—that knowledge of Shakespeare makes for right conduct or that familiarity with the universe will put an end to human ills and discontent.

Sharing so much, the sciences and the humanities must therefore now conclude a new partnership on behalf of all knowledge and understanding. The communities of both—though the community of the humanities remains far less organized—should become more closely involved at all levels and in all pursuits. For without joint efforts—intellectual, institutional, and civic—both will suffer and, along with them, American culture will suffer, too.

—James M. Banner, JR., *Chairman, American Association for the Advancement of the Humanities, 918 16th Street, NW, Washington, D.C. 20006.*

This editorial appeared in *Science*, January 2, 1981, and is reprinted with permission.

Appendix III

Usefulness of the Social Sciences

National attention has turned to the productivity, the performance, and even the profitability of science. Measured against such criteria, how will the social sciences fare? Quite well, I believe. Close scrutiny will disclose substantial contributions to economic growth and the public welfare. For instance, numerous well-established industries now market technologies that are derived from social science research: demographic projections, programmed language instruction, standardized educational testing, behavior modification, man-machine system design, political polling, consumer research

139

market testing, management consulting. Just as medicine draws upon biological research or electronics upon physics, government and management draw upon psychology, economics, demography, geography, and other social sciences.

In addition, the social sciences have vastly extended the observational powers of contemporary societies. Advanced industrial nations are commonly described as information societies in reference to their systematically collected information about the human as well as the physical environment. Human actions and the meanings attached to them constitute the most dynamic and complex of all those environments in which markets sell, banks invest, businesses produce, governments govern, and families plan. Monitoring the ever-changing human environment is a task approached through a variety of tools and disciplines of the social sciences: economic indicators, demographic trends, national statistical systems, historical research, time-series analysis, input-output matrices, developmental psychology, area studies, political geography.

Of course, the public importance of the social sciences, like that of the biological and physical sciences, is not limited to the accomplishments as observational sciences or to a list of industries that market their technologies. It is through theories and intellectual constructs that the sciences realize their greatest potential. In the empirical regularities they reveal, the counterintuitive questions they ask, the contingent associations they discover, and the successive layers of meaning they uncover, the social sciences conceptualize and thereby render accessible to human intelligence a wide array of economic, social, political, and cultural phenomena. Ironically, the social sciences seldom get full credit for their theoretical accomplishments, because the discoveries, once labeled, are quickly absorbed into conventional wisdom. This is easily demonstrated; note the number of social science concepts common to our vocabulary: human capital, gross national product, identity crisis, span of control, the unconscious, price elasticity, acculturation, political party identification reference group, externalities. Obviously, the phenomena revealed through such concepts existed prior to the relevant research, just as DNA, quarks, and the source of the Nile existed prior to their discovery. Yet concepts generated through research are discoveries that make phenomena intelligible and accessible that previously were inaccurately or incompletely understood.

That the tools and concepts of social science work their way into public discourse is a matter of some national importance. Regulatory policy, for example, is seldom discussed without reference to cost-benefit analysis. It is with models from economics and demography that the financial base of Social Security is being examined. Evaluation research is called upon to demonstrate program successes or failures. Game theory provides a vocabulary for looking at shifting international alliances. The current national discussion of productivity will make use of research on topics such as investment and savings behavior, management of complex organizations, competency testing, international labor migration, or human creativity.

In just a few decades the social sciences have accomplished much of practical significance. With continued public and private support, much can reasonably be expected in the decades to come.

—Kenneth Prewitt, *President, Social Science Research Council, 605 Third Avenue, New York 10016.*

Science, February 13, 1981. Reprinted with permission.

Appendix IV

Science and Ethics:
Can They Be Reconnected?

In that branch of contemporary philosophy called ethics, "science"—or at least "the natural and social sciences" as they are conceived of in the English-speaking world—receives very little attention.

And yet, interactions between science and ethics were once vigorous and cordial.

How have science and ethics become estranged? And how, in an era in which the two must inevitably collide, can they be put on speaking terms again?

From a strict philosophical point of view, all attempts to insulate the sciences from ethics can be easily undercut. This is true whether we discuss the basic concepts of the sciences, the institutions and collective conduct of the scientific profession, or the personal motives of individual scientists.

As to the concept of science: so long as we restrict ourselves to the physical and chemical sciences, our basic notions and hypotheses (e.g., hadron, field gradient, and amino acid) may have no obvious evaluative implications. But the physiological, to say nothing of the psychological and social sciences, employ whole families of concepts, such as functionality and adaptedness, and their cognates, which raise evaluative issues directly.

As to the scientific profession: the codes of good intellectual practice, and the criteria of professional judgment in the sciences, may once upon a time have looked to the needs of effective inquiry alone, rather than to broader "ethical" considerations. But it is by now no longer possible to draw so clear or sharp a line between the intellectual demands of good science and the ethical demands of the good life. The increasingly close links between basic science and its practical applications expose working scientists more and more to ethical problems and public accountability of sorts that are commonplace in service professions such as medicine and law.

Finally, as to the individual motives that operate for scientists in their work: though the ideal spring of action for scientific inquiry may be a pure respect for the rationality of the inquiry itself, such a pure respect is at best an aspiration, and a *moral* aspiration at that. Furthermore, it is something that can be developed in the course of any individual's lifetime only as a somewhat refined product of moral education.

Yet, despite these powerful objections, the notion that the intellectual activities of science are carried on at a level that sets them, if not above, then at any rate beside and on a par with the moral law, continues to have its charms; and we must try to understand its seductive power. One potent source, I suggest, has been scientists' fear of relativism. Recognition of anthropological diversity led, by around 1800, to a widespread sense—not by any means confined to philosophers—that ethical beliefs and practices vary arbitrarily from culture to culture. Earlier in the eighteenth century it had still been possible for Voltaire to declare, "There is only one morality, as there is only one geometry"; but, from 1800 on, cultural relativism became a force to reckon with in general thinking about ethical matters.

Since this relativism and subjectivism put the very foundations of ethics in doubt, it was understandable that scientists should have resisted the intrusion of ethics into the business of science; and that, in return, they should have insisted that the concerns of science— unlike those of ethics—were entirely objective, and in no sense "matters of taste or feeling." Furthermore, the fact that scientific issues could plausibly be depicted as public and intersubjective (i.e., "rational") made it possible, also, to define the intellectual demands of the scientific life in a similarly objective way. So, both the collective conduct of the scientific profession and the personal choices of individual scientists were apparently freed from the existential arbitrariness and ambiguity of the ethical realm.

At this point, it might have been better if philosophers and scientists alike had emphasized the similarities between science and ethics, and had used the "rational objectivity" of science as a model in seeking to reestablish the claims of moral objectivity. The argument that ethical issues are, in their own proper ways, as public and intersubjective as scientific issues (and so equally "rational") was thus abandoned too quickly and lightly. But many scientists, lacking any sense of joint intellectual responsibility and interest with the moral philosophers, were happy enough to disown relativism in science and bolt for cover on their own. For so long as relativism and subjectivism remained viable options in philosophical ethics, most scientists understandably felt that it was more important to emphasize the distinctively intellectual—and so, presumably, "value-neutral"—character of their own enterprises. Provided they could preserve the autonomy of the scientific community against all outsiders they did not mind letting the moral philosophers sink or swim by themselves.

By now, however, the "rationality" of science—the objectivity of scientific issues, the autonomy of the scientific professions, and the categorical claims of the scientific life—can no longer be used to differentiate science entirely from the rest of thought and morality. We are faced, on every level, not by a hard and fast distinction, but by a spectrum.

- The basic concepts of the sciences range along a spectrum from the effectively "value-free" to the irretrievably "value-laden";
- The goals of the scientific enterprise range along the spectrum

from a purely abstract interest in theoretical speculations to a
direct concern with human good and ill;
- The professional responsibilities of the scientific community
  range along a spectrum from the strictly internal and intellectual
  to the most public and practical.

Nonetheless, as recently as the 1930s, when I first acquired my ideas
about "science," the most characteristic mark of the scientific attitude and the scientific task was to select as one's preferred center of
attention the purest, the most intellectual, the most autonomous, and
the least ethically implicated extreme on each of these different
spectrums.

   No doubt this "puristic" view of science was an extreme one, and
by no means universally shared by working scientists, to say nothing
of the outside social commentators who wrote about the scientific
scene. Yet it is a view that had, and continues to have, great attractions for many professional scientists. Since "rational objectivity" is
an indispensable part of the scientific mission, and the intrusion of
"values" into science had come to be regarded as incompatible with
such objectivity, all concern with values (or other arbitrary, personal
preferences) had to be foresworn in the higher interest of rationality.
Certainly, the professional institutions of science tended to be organized on this basis. The memberships of scientific academies, for
instance, have for the last 75 or 100 years been increasingly recruited
on the basis of the narrowly defined intellectual contributions of
candidates alone, without regard to their social perceptiveness, ethical sensitivity, or political wisdom. Indeed, the puristic view is still
powerful today: consider, for instance, the recent proposals by
Arthur Kantrowitz of M.I.T. for a Science Court, whose duty would
be to pronounce on the "factual implications" of science and technology for issues of public policy, without reference to the "values" at
stake in each case.

   Accordingly, the purism of the views about science into which I
was initiated was not merely a feature of the particular culture and
time of my youth: one more local and temporary characteristic of the
factual, unemotional, antiphilosophical, class-structured, and role-
oriented attitudes of the English professional classes between the two
world wars. Many of the considerations advanced to explain and
justify scientific purism—the intellectual reaction against ethical

relativism, the collective desire for professional autonomy, the personal charms of an ethically unambiguous life plan—have a force that carries them across national boundaries.

What deeper explanation should we look for, then, to account for the emergence of this puristic view of science? Granted that, by the early twentieth century, relativism and subjectivism were beginning to pose an implicit threat to the objectivity of science as well as to ethics, how was it that scientists perceived and defined their own collective interests and self-image so clearly? How did they come to suppose that they could see science as capable of being the stronghold of reason by itself and on its own, in contradistinction to ethics, which had seemingly been unmasked as the plaything of emotion?

The distinction between an objective science and a subjective ethics may be traced back at least as far as the scientific positivism of Comte, in the early nineteenth century—i.e., the belief that science can be built up from scratch by only a dispassionate observer, starting from the same repertory of morally neutral "facts" about the world. The same contrast helped to encourage the revival of scientific positivism in Vienna in the 1920s. But why was scientific positivism itself able to carry conviction from the early nineteenth century on, in a way that it had not done earlier?

I believe the crucial development in the history of nineteenth-century science was the establishment of distinct scientific disciplines, professions, and roles: that is, the process by which individual, sharply delimited special sciences began to crystallize from the larger and less-defined matrix of eighteenth-century natural philosophy. As a result of this change, scientific workers divided themselves up into new and self-organized collectivities, and acquired a collective consciousness of their specialized intellectual tasks, as contrasted with the broader concerns of philosophical, literary, and theological discussion more generally. In this way, it at last became possible to define the new individual role of "scientist." (This familiar word was coined as recently as 1840 by William Whewell, on the model of the much older term "artist," for his presidential address to the British Association for the Advancement of Science.)

In these respects, scientific roles and writings, organizations and arguments dating from before 1830 differ sharply from anything to be found after around 1890. In the hands of the most distinguished eighteenth-century authors, scientific issues were always expanding into, and merging with, broader intellectual questions. In the writings of a John Ray or a Joseph Priestley, the doors between science, ethics, and religion are always open. "And why not?" they would have asked; "for natural philosophy must surely embrace within itself, not just mathematical and experimental philosophy, but also natural theology and natural morality." (Their sentiments were also those of Isaac Newton himself, for whom "to discourse of God" from a study of His Creation "does certainly belong to natural philosophy.") Indeed, it took a series of deliberate and collective decisions to restrict the scope of scientific debate before these larger issues of philosophy and theology were effectively excluded from the professional debate about scientific issues. One such example was the resolution adopted by the Geological Society of London in 1807 to exclude from its Proceedings all arguments about the origin, antiquity, and creation of the earth, as being merely speculative, and to confine the Proceedings to papers based on direct observations of the earth's crust. During the rest of the nineteenth century, the intellectual concerns of the different special sciences were identified and defined in progressively sharper terms, setting them apart from the broader interests of philosophers, theologians, and the general reading public.

At this point, we should look at the manner in which natural philosophy, as conceived in the seventeenth and eighteenth centuries, fell apart into its component elements, and the sciences (and scientists) were led to set up shop on their own. Even as late as the 1820s, Joseph Townsend could still present significant contributions to geological science in the guise of an argument vindicating *The Veracity of Moses as an Historian*. By the end of the century, Biblical history and geochronology had become entirely distinct disciplines, pursued by quite separate communities of scholars. Yet, even in this case, the transitions involved were protracted, hard-fought, and painful. Similarly, one major reason for the hostile reception that greeted Darwin's *Origin of Species* was the threat it seemingly posed to the traditional association between natural history and sacred history. Acknowledging a presentation copy of the book, Darwin's teacher Adam Sedgwick expressed sorrow and alarm at Darwin's disregard of the "essential link" between the moral and material order of the world. If natural historians no longer showed us how the hand of the Creator was exemplified in the living creatures that were

His handiwork, how then could the human race be expected to retain its confidence in Divine wisdom and providence?

In addition, we might examine the institutional changes during the nineteenth century by the leading scientific academies and societies that had originally been founded from 1650 on. How did they move from being general associations of scholars, clerics, and gentlemen to being specialized organizations of professional experts, with a narrowly defined scope and strict entrance qualifications? Before 1830, the Royal Society of London was still largely an association for the general discussion of issues in natural philosophy. Even in the second half of the nineteenth century, it was still accepted as a matter of common form that a poet such as Alfred Tennyson should be a Fellow of the Royal Society, and sit on important Royal Society committees. By the 1890s, it had become the mode to pursue, not just art for art's sake, but also science for science's sake, even, electrical theory for electrical theory's sake, organic chemistry for organic chemistry's sake, botanical taxonomy for botanical taxonomy's sake. This was so because, by 1890, the self-defining disciplines and autonomous professions with which we are familiar today—each of them devoted to the special aims of one or another science—had finally established an existence independent of each other.

Once again, however, these institutional claims did not come automatically or easily. On the contrary, the intellectual and institutional claims of the special sciences faced continued resistance from the churches and elsewhere. So the collective experience, interests, and self-perceptions of, for example, cell physiologists, historical geologists, and electromagnetic theorists led them to defend their newly won territories with some real jealousy, to act protectively toward the intellectual goals of their disciplines, and to resist any countermoves aimed at reabsorbing them into some larger system of philosophy or theology.

In short, to understand how science came to part company from the foundations of ethics, we need to examine the history of scientific specialization. It was the development of specialization and professionalization that was responsible for excluding ethical issues from the foundations of science, and so, though inadvertently, destroyed most of the links between science and the foundations of ethics. During the hundred or so years beginning around 1840, the concepts and methods, collective organization, and individual roles of science were progressively sharpened and defined, in ways designed to insulate truly "scientific" issues and investigations from all external distractions. So defined, the task of "positive science" was to reveal how and in what respects, regardless of whether we like them or not, discoverable regularities, connections, and mechanisms are manifest in, or responsible for, the phenomena of the natural world.

This "positive" program for science was sometimes associated, but was never identical, with the philosophy of scientific positivism. It rested on the following assumptions.

A scientific picture of the world differs radically from a metaphysico-religious picture. The former is realistically confined to demonstrable facts about the natural world: the latter embeds those demonstrable facts within a larger conceptual system, structured according to prejudices that are (from the scientific standpoint) arbitrary, externally motivated, and presumably wish-fulfilling.

A realistic view of the natural world is one that is kept free of irrelevant preferences and evaluations, and so depicts Nature as it is, "whether we like it or not."

If scientific work is to be effectively organized and prosecuted, questions of "demonstrable fact" must be investigated quite separately from all arbitrary, external, wish-fulfilling notions. Only in this way can we carry forward the technical inquiries of science proper, without being sidetracked into fruitless and inconclusive debates about rival values or *Weltanschauungen* to which individual scientists may happen (like anyone else) to be attracted for personal reasons.

Thus, the deeper reasons for defining the scope and procedures of the special sciences in ways that keep ethical issues out of their foundations were connected with the basic methodological program of the modern scientific movement. In particular, they reflect the steps which have been taken over the last 100 years to give institutional expression to the maxims and ambitions of the founders of the Royal Society, through the professionalization of the scientific enterprise. Given the care and effort that the community of professional scientists has taken in this way to insulate the foundations of science from ethics, we should not therefore be surprised if they have made it that much harder to preserve clear and significant connections between science and the foundations of ethics, as well.

In all these ways, nineteenth-century natural scientists worked to keep ethical considerations and preferences from operating within "the foundations of science"; so that, for instance, the tests for deciding whether one scientific theory or concept was "better" or "worse" than its rivals, from the scientific point of view, should be wholly divorced from issues about what was ethically "better" or "worse." It was a matter of great importance for them to be able to make the choice between alternative theories or concepts turn solely on "objective" or "factual" considerations: thus, they could avoid having to face the question whether one theory or concept is morally preferable to, or more objectionable than, rival theories or concepts.

That kind of value neutrality was, of course, quite compatible with particular scientists adopting all sorts of ethical views and positions on their own responsibility. It was even compatible with one rather more general, collective view: namely, that we must begin by drawing a sharp line between matters of pure or real science and matters of applied science or—more precisely—of technology, after which it will become clear that questions of ethical desirability can arise only in the latter, technological area. (To put it crudely, anatomy is value-free, clinical medicine value-laden.) Above all, it was compatible with all sorts of philosophical discussions, as professional scientists sought to rationalize or justify their particular ethical positions, and square their personal views about ethics with their scientific interests and methodologies.

In our own day, however, the accumulated successes of the "positive" methodology have carried science—and scientists—up against the limits of that program's validity, and in some places across them. To begin to answer my central question—"How can we set about reconnecting the sciences with the foundations of ethics?"—let us identify certain points at which, during the last few years, the location of these limits has become apparent.

> *The positive program for science normally took for granted a sentimental view of ethics: this was used to justify excluding ethics—which was assumed to deal with labile and subjective matters of taste or feeling—from the systematic investigation of "demonstrable facts." It was assumed, in other words, that human values, valuations and preferences have no place within the world of nature that is the scientist's object of study.*

During the twentieth century, by contrast, science has expanded into the realms of physiology and psychology, and in so doing has shown the limits of that assumption. As physiology and psychology have succeeded in securing their own positions as sciences, human beings have ceased to be onlookers contemplating a natural world to which they themselves are foreign and have become parts of (or participants within) that world. As a result, the makeup, operations, and activities of human beings themselves have become legitimate issues for scientific investigation. At the very least, the biochemical and physiological preconditions of *normal* functioning, and so of *good* health, can accordingly be discussed nowadays as problems for science, as well as for ethics. With this crucial incursion by science into the foundations of ethics, we can recognize that not all *human* evaluations must necessarily be regarded, from the scientific point of view, as *irrelevant* evaluations. On the contrary, some of the processes and phenomena studied by natural sciences carry with them certain immediate evaluative implications for the "good and ill" of human life. With this example before us, we are ready to take the first step in the direction hinted at earlier: that of using the "rational objectivity" of science as a model for reestablishing the claims of moral objectivity.

> *Given the increasingly close involvement of basic science with its applications to human welfare, notably in the area of medical research, it is meanwhile becoming clear that the professional organization and priorities of scientific work can no longer be concerned solely with considerations of intellectual content and merit, as contrasted with the ethical acceptability and social value, either of the research process itself, or of its practical consequences.*

The very existence of the bioethics movement is one indication of this change. The work of the National Commmission for the Protection of Human Subjects, and of institutional review boards to review research involving human subjects, is another.

This being the case, the doors between science and the foundations of ethics can no longer be kept bolted from the scientific side, as they were in the heyday of positive science. Neither the disciplinary aspects of the sciences, their basic concepts and intellectual methods, nor the professional aspects of scientific work, the collective organization of science and its criteria of professional judgment, can ever again be insulated against the "extraneous and irrelevant" influence of ethics, values, and preferences.

On what conditions, then, can we reestablish the frayed links between science and ethics?

1. We should not attempt to reestablish these links by reviving outworn styles of natural theology. The kind of syncretistic cosmology to be found in Teilhard de Chardin, for example, is no improvement on its predecessors: this is indeed an area in which "demonstrable facts" are in real danger of being obscured by a larger wish-fulfilling framework of theological fantasies. Instead, we should embark on a critical scientific and philosophical reexamination of humanity's place in nature, with special reference to the use of such terms as "function" and "adaptation," behind which the ethical aspects of our involvement in the natural world are too easily concealed.

2. We should not insist on seeing ethical significance in all of science, let alone require that every piece of scientific investigation should have a demonstrable human relevance. Though the enthusiasms of the 1960s "counterculture" were intelligible enough in their historical context, that would be going too far in the opposite direction, and would land us in worse trouble than the positivist program itself. Instead, we should pay critical attention to the respects in which, and the points at which, ethical issues enter into the conduct of scientific work, including its immediate practical consequences. The ethical aspects of human experimentation, and of such enterprises as sex research, are only samples from a much larger group of possible issues.

3. We should not see this renewed interaction between science and ethics as threatening, or justifying, any attack on the proper autonomy of scientists within their own specific professional domains. The recent debate about recombinant DNA research generated rhetoric of two contrary kinds; both from scientists who saw the whole affair as a pretext for outside interference in the proper affairs of the scientific professions, and from laypersons who genuinely believed that those affairs were being carried on irresponsibly. Instead, we should reconsider, in a more selective way, just what the proper scope and limits of professional autonomy are, and at what points scientists cross the line separating legitimate professional issues from matters of proper public concern, whether political or ethical.

4. We should not suppose that renewing diplomatic relations between science and ethics will do anything to throw doubt on the virtues, duties, and obligations of the scientific role or station. During the last fifteen years, the anti-scientific excesses of the radicals have sometimes made it appear necessary to apologize for being a scientist; and, as a reaction against this radical rhetoric, some professional scientists have developed, in turn, a kind of resentful truculence toward public discussions about the ethical and political involvements of the scientific life. Instead, we need to understand better how the lines between the narrowly professional and broader social responsibilities of scientists run in the collective sphere, and also how individual scientists can balance their obligations within the overall demands of a morally acceptable life, as between their chosen professional roles as neurophysiologists, for example, and the other obligations to which they are subject in other capacities as citizens, colleagues, lovers, parents, religious believers, or whatever.

During the last few years, the "purist" view of science—as a strictly autonomous intellectual enterprise, insulated against the influence of all merely human needs, wishes, and preferences—has thus lost its plausibility. Whether we consider the basic concepts of the sciences, the collective enterprises of professional science, or the personal commitments and motivations of individual scientists, we can maintain a strictly value-free (or rather, ethics-free) position only by sticking arbitrarily to one extreme end of a long spectrum.

From that extreme point of view, the ideally scientific investigation would be a piece of strictly academic research on some application-proof project in theoretical physics, conducted by a friendless and stateless bachelor of independent means. There may have been a substantial body of science approximating this ideal as recently as the 1880s and 1890s, but that is certainly not the case any longer. On the contrary, we can learn something about the foundations of ethics by reconsidering the character and content of the scientific enterprise on all three levels.

1. As a collective activity, any science is significant for ethics because of the ways in which it serves as an embodiment or exemplar of applied rationality. In this respect, the very objectivity of the goals at which scientists aim, both collectively and individually, provides us with the starting point for a counterattack against relativism and subjectivism in ethics, too.

2. Correspondingly, the moral character of the scientists's personal motivation, particularly the way in which the Kantian "pure respect for rationality as such" grows out of the wider life of affect or "inclination"—what I have elsewhere called "the moral psychology of science"—can teach us something about the nature of personal virtue and commitment in other areas of life.

3. Finally, the actual content of the sciences is at last contributing to a better understanding of the human locus within the natural world. This fact is well recognized in the physiological sciences, where the links between *normal* functioning and *good* health are comparatively unproblematic. But it is a matter of active dispute in several areas just at this time: for example, in the conflict over the relations between social psychology and sociobiology. And there are some other fields in which it should be the topic of much more active debate than it is: for example, in connection with the rivalry between psychotherapeutic and psychopharmacological modes of treatment in psychiatry.

This done, it should not be hard to indicate the points at which issues originating in the natural sciences can give rise to, and grow together with, evaluative issues—and not merely with issues that involve the values "intrinsic to" the scientific enterprise itself, but also larger human values of a more strictly ethical kind. For as we saw, the new phase of scientific development into which we are now moving requires us to reinsert human observers into the world of nature, so that we become not merely onlookers, but also participants in many of the natural phenomena and processes that are subject matter of our scientific investigations. This is true across the whole spectrum of late twentieth-century science: all the way from quantum mechanics, where Heisenberg's Principle requires us to acknowledge the interdependence of the oberserver and the observed, to ecology, where the conduct of human beings is one crucial factor in any causal analysis of the condition of, say, Lake Erie, or to psychiatry, where the two-way interaction between the psychiatrist and his client is in sharp contrast to the one-way influence of nature on the human observer (but not *vice versa*) presupposed in classical nineteenth-century science.

Recognizing the interconnectedness of human conduct and natural phenomena may not by itself determine the direction in which those interconnections should point us. Admitting the need to establish some harmony between human conduct and natural processes is one thing: agreeing on what constitutes such a harmony is another, harder task. There was, for instance, a disagreement between Thomas Henry Huxley and his grandson, Julian, about the relations between human ethics and organic evolution. T.H. saw it as a basic human obligation to fight against the cruelty and destructiveness of natural selection, whereas Julian saw the direction of human progress as a simple continuation of the direction of organic evolution. What both Huxleys agreed about, however, was the need to see human ethics as having a place in the world of nature, and to arrive at a rational understanding of what that relation is.

It was with this need in mind that I referred to such concepts as function and adaptation as requiring particular scutiny. For the question, "What is the true *function* of human beings?" is potentially as much a topic of debate today as it was in classical Athens, when Plato had Socrates raise it in the *Republic*. Likewise, the question, "How should our ways of acting change, in order to become *better adapted* to the novel situations in which we are finding ourselves?" is a question that also invites answers—sometimes, overly simple answers—based on a reading of contemporary biology and ecology. For better and for worse, we are probably ripe for a revival of the organic theory of society and the state. And, though this is a topic that must be taken seriously, it is also one that is going to need to be handled with great caution and subtlety, if we are to avoid the crudely conservative emphases of earlier versions of the theory. Starting from where we do, the answers we give to such questions will certainly need to be richer and more complex than those available in Plato's time; but, sharing Plato's questions, we are evidently back in a situation where our view of ethics and our view of nature are coming back together again.

> —Stephen Toulmin, *Professor in the Department of Philosophy and the Divinity School at the University of Chicago.*

> This article, adapted from an article in the *The Hasting Center Report*, June 1979, appeared in the *University of Chicago Magazine*, Winter 1981 (© *The University of Chicago*) and is reprinted here with permission.

Index

Mind-stuff—*see Gedankenstoffe*
M'Naghten Rule, 81
Monkeys,
  and random typing, 103
Montessori education, 127
Montessori, Maria, 127
Morowitz, Harold J., 38, 115, 129

Napoleon, 121
Nature,
  grand scheme of, 26, 27, 55
Newton, Isaac, 64, 100, 148
Non-material—*see Gedankenstoffe*,
  material, unseen
Nutrients, 27, 41, 45, 70
Nutrition,
  and health, 45
  and reproduction, 50, 71, 72
Nutritional diseases, 28, 29, 46, 47, 50

Orthomolecular psychiatry and medicine, 24, 46

Pantothenic acid, 28, 46, 51
Parry of Bath, 111
Pauling, Linus, 24, 46
Peace, 59, 119
People,
  nature of, 74
Physics, 64, 82, 126
Pinkel, Benjamin, 115
Planck, Max, 57
Plato, 79, 156
Pope, Alexander, 14
Positivism,
  scientific, 147, 150
Prewitt, Kenneth, 141
Priestley, Joseph, 148
Prigogine, Ilya, 39, 116
Psychodes, 30, 105
Psychology, 76, 120, 126, 152
  differential, 127

men vs. women, 121

Quakers, 105, 120

Ray, John, 148
Religion, 37, 57, 58, 107, 115-18, 120, 134, 148
Rockefeller Foundation Commission
  on the Humanities, 20, 39, 56, 129, 133, 135
Royal Society of London, 150

Science,
  interrelations with humanities, 20, 55, 129, 134, 135, 143
Sedgwick, Adam, 148
Shakespeare, William, 23
Shaw, George Bernard, 25
Slavery, 105
Smith, John E., 116, 129
Snow, C.P., 56
Social problems, 49, 54
Social Science Research Council, 141
Social sciences, 49, 129, 139, 143
Socrates, 79, 95, 156
Solar system, 63, 65
Specialization, scientific,
  history of, 149
Spencer, Herbert, 5
Stevenson, Robert Lewis, 99

Teaching profession, 58, 125
Teilhard de Chardin, Pierre, 153
Tennyson, A fred, 149
Thurston, L. L., 77
Toulmin, Stephen, 156
Townsend, Joseph, 148
Twain, Mark, 19

Unified education, 9, 15, 17, 34, 43, 58, 88, 113, 114, 121, 123
University of Texas, 14, 42